THE GREAT TEAMS

Why They Win All the Time

THE
GREAT TEAMS
Why They Win All the Time

by ROBERT A. LISTON

Doubleday & Company, Inc., Garden City, New York

Library of Congress Cataloging in Publication Data

Liston, Robert A
The great teams.

Bibliography: p. 235.
1. Athletic clubs—United States—History.
2. Sports—United States—History.   3. Group games.
I. Title.
GV583.L57   796′.06′0973
ISBN: 0-385-03590-X Trade
0-385-03620-5 Prebound
Library of Congress Catalog Card Number 78–20081

To Wes and Marion Eastman

ACKNOWLEDGMENTS

The byline may carry a single name, but writing a book is also a team effort. Many people contributed. I would like to thank Larry Wahl of the New York Yankees; Howie McHugh of the Boston Celtics; Wilt Browning of the Baltimore Colts; Marv Homan of Ohio State University; Mark Dillon of UCLA; Claude Mutoh of the Montreal Canadiens; J. T. Barber of Raybestos-Manhattan, Inc.; and Doug Todd of the Dallas Cowboys. Special thanks go to Patricia Cooper; Stephen W. Liston; the capable and long-suffering staff of the Marvin Memorial Library in Shelby, Ohio; and to my daughter, Felicia Liston. My wife, Jean, had the onerous task of correcting the manuscript.

R.A.L.
Shelby, Ohio

CONTENTS

SOMETHING MORE THAN TALENT   1

NEW YORK YANKEES   9
A Matter of Character   10

BOSTON CELTICS   40
Their Thing in Boston   41

BALTIMORE COLTS   62
The Importance of Leadership   64

UCLA BRUINS   87
A Certain Selflessness   89

OHIO STATE BUCKEYES   113
How to Build a Machine   114

MONTREAL CANADIENS   134

    The Importance of Fans   135

DALLAS COWBOYS   154

    Organizing to Win   155

RAYBESTOS BRAKETTES   181

    The Will to Win   183

OAKLAND A'S   203

    The Madder They Got   205

WHAT MAKES A TEAM?   225

READINGS   235

INDEX   237

THE GREAT TEAMS

Why They Win All the Time

SOMETHING MORE THAN TALENT

"Gimme a T. Gimme an E. Gimme an A. Gimme an M.
RAH TEAM!"
"Two, four, six, eight, who do we appreciate?
TEAM! TEAM! TEAM!"

In such ways, led by cheerleaders, do we exhort our sports teams on to victory. At crucial moments in a game, we bellow ourselves hoarse commanding the players to either "Go, Team, Go" or "Defense! Defense!"

We are interested in such individualistic sports as boxing and golf, horseracing and chess, but most of our time, interest, and money is lavished upon team sports, especially baseball, basketball, football, softball, and hockey. Is it ever! There is really no way to compute attendance at these sports. They are played from grade school through high school and college, and there are, of course, various semi-pro and professional leagues. We go to Pop Warner and midget football games and Little League, Babe Ruth, and American Legion baseball games. In Canada, junior and senior hockey attract large crowds. Nor is it possible to compute the billions of tax and private dollars spent on tickets, stadiums and arenas and gymnasiums, bats and balls and other equipment, coaches and players and salaried executives to run the teams and sports programs, as well as TV networks, stations, and sets to watch our favorite teams.

Yes, we certainly do like our team sports. Not a few of the more philosophical have wondered and worried about this. Our craze for sports spectacles has been likened to gladiator contests in ancient Rome, with some seeing our absorption in sports as a sign of our decadence. Others see our fanaticism about such violent sports as football and hockey as a useful sublimation of our own violent natures. As society becomes more peaceful and orderly, we need outlets for our aggression. Hence our interest in sports— supposedly. Then there are the worries about our own health. We spend so much time as spectators, either at the games or glued to the television set, that we are not getting enough exercise ourselves.

And there are concerns about the effects of team sports on family life. So many hours are spent watching sports on Saturday and Sunday afternoons and weekday evenings that wives are said to feel neglected. So much money and glory is lavished upon successful athletes that sons are being urged to grow up to be a quarterback rather than President. To push young children into a competitive cauldron is said to be bad for them. Nonsense, say others. Competitive sports build character.

Whatever the pros and cons of these arguments, the simple fact is that Americans love team sports and lavish an immense amount of attention and money on them.

Team. Be a member of the team. Work together as a team. Teamwork. These ideas have spread into areas of American life far removed from playing fields. In the armed

forces, in our giant corporations, retail stores, and government offices, people are organized into units frequently
called "teams" and set to competing against similar "teams"
to build or sell more items or outperform in some way.
Leaders in many walks of life, even in the White House,
urge those under them to be members of the team.

Yet for all our interest in team sports and all our talk
about teamwork, we know very little about the ingredients
that make a team. What is teamwork? Better said, how is a
team of people made to work together? How are five or six
or nine or eleven persons, all highly talented individuals in
their own right, made to jell into a unit that wins games?
How are they induced to co-operate for victory, to surrender their egos, their moment of glory, their individual pride
for a collective goal? Why are certain teams so successful
year after year, while other teams languish as also-rans,
never coming even close to winning a pennant or entering a
playoff?

A quick answer is that the successful teams have the best
players. That is simply often not the case. Talented players
are needed to win, but there is something far more elusive
at work on the great teams. Every team in every sport has
some outstanding players, frequently many of them, yet
they are not consistent winners. For many years, Tom Yawkey spent fortunes trying to make his Boston Red Sox a
baseball dynasty. Yet between 1947 and 1967 his teams
could not win a pennant. Former movie star Gene Autry
has spent lavishly trying to make his California Angels a
champion, but has thus far been frustrated. In the late
1960s and early 1970s, the Oakland Raiders were the winningest team in professional football, yet failed to become
Super Bowl champions until 1977. The team they beat, the
Minnesota Vikings, have failed so often in the Super Bowl

or on the way to it that a person almost weeps for their frustration.

It is axiomatic in sports that the team that wins may not have the best players. Consider the "no name" defensive team of the Miami Dolphins, twice Super Bowl champions. Remember that aging Green Bay team, its best years behind them, which roused itself to defeat a young, strong Dallas Cowboy team and go on to another championship. Remember, too, that fantastic Boston Celtics team, its key members considered old and over the hill, getting it together one more time to win another title. The New York Yankees won five World Series in a row with a team that was considerably inferior to previous Yankee teams and probably wasn't the best team in baseball. Yet they won and won and won. How did they do it? How do the great teams manage to win despite injuries and adversity and "bad luck"? When things get tough, the great teams get tougher. Many words are applied to these qualities—pride, spirit, teamwork—but really what are these things? And if they are important to victory, where do these qualities come from?

In a quest for answers, I have studied a number of great sports teams, talking to coaches, managers, players, and others associated with the team. The basic questions were: How do you make a team? What made your team great? The answers, all quite varied, are both illuminating and surprising. I, for one, learned a lot.

Which teams? I chose teams in professional baseball, basketball, football, and hockey, and in college football and basketball. These are the most popular team sports in the United States. College, high school, sandlot, and Little League baseball thrive, but they do not usually attract huge crowds of spectators. For the same reason I eliminated such minor sports as lacrosse. Track attracts huge audiences and we speak of track teams, but track is really individual performances, man against man, woman against woman. Only in passing the baton in relays do track performers cooperate or interact with each other. The same may be said of swimming teams. Tennis, too.

Reluctantly, I eliminated soccer. It is the most popular sport in the world, one calling for superb teamwork. For a variety of reasons, it has not caught on in the United States, although interest is growing and there is hope for the future. At this point, however, there is no American soccer team that can be ranked with the great foreign teams.

In selecting the specific teams for study, I looked for those to which the word "dynastic" might be applied. They field consistently strong teams over a number of years. They either win the championship or are in the playoffs. Said another way, if they don't win, they scare those who do. They seem victorious no matter what. They lose star players, even whole teams of players, and go on winning. They change coaches and managers, even owners, and still win. They may drop down a year or two while they rebuild, but soon they are back at the top. These teams create dynasties.

These criteria hardly made the selection of teams easy. Perhaps no one team fulfills all of them. Of the nine teams described in this book, the selection of five will be obvious to all sports fans. The New York Yankees, the Boston Celtics, the Montreal Canadiens, the Raybestos Brakettes, and the UCLA Bruins in college basketball have been dynastic in every sense of the word. The other four choices were arbitrary on my part. Few will quarrel with the fact that the Baltimore Colts, Dallas Cowboys, and Ohio State Buckeyes in football have been dynastic. But why choose them? Dozens of others are just as good or better. An often important factor in the choice was geography. I did not want more than one team from the same area. I could, for example, have chosen four teams from Los Angeles. The Dodgers in baseball, the Rams in football, UCLA in basketball, and the Southern California Trojans in college football are all dynastic. The ninth team selected is the Oakland A's. It is here because as a team the A's did just about the exact opposite of all the other great teams, yet won three World Series in a row.

What is teamwork? How is it achieved? Each of the teams described here does it a bit differently. The coaches and players, even the owners, offer different reasons for the success of their teams. Yet there are common answers, similar methods. An attempt is made to sum up these in the last chapter.

Here in the beginning we should ponder the essential paradox in any team activity. A player on a team is asked to give his all as an individual and to excel as an individual, yet work together as a team. That is not at all easy, for the two tend to be opposites. The very act of excelling as an individual would seem to mean non-co-operation with your teammates. How can a person be asked to excel individually yet sacrifice himself for the good of the team? The two would not seem to go together, yet that is exactly what happens on the great teams. Indeed, the ability to resolve this essential paradox consistently is what separates the consistent winners from the also-rans.

One other observation. We admire the great teams. We cheer the whole team to victory. Yet we honor and glorify the individuals. We say the pitcher won the game. Actually, all he did was contribute. The other eight players on the diamond had to field the ball and they had to score runs. In the American League, the pitcher doesn't even bat and thus help to score runs. We say the quarterback completed the pass or the running back scored a touchdown. But it took ten other guys to contribute to that completion or that score. They had to fend off the pass rush or open a hole in the line for the runner.

The individual sports stars all know this. It is a team effort. O. J. Simpson, the celebrated back for the Buffalo Bills and now San Francisco, has won respect not only for his great running but also because he invariably attributes his success to the offensive linemen who block for him. The offensive linemen in football are probably the most unsung people in sports. Sportcasters and sportswriters do their best to mention them by name from time to time, but they seldom get much glory. There are statistics galore on pass completions and receptions and interceptions, yards gained, points scored, punts, and returns of kicks. Tallies are kept of how many tackles a defensive player makes or how many times the quarterback is sacked. But there are no statistics on offensive blocks. Only the player himself and the coaches who watch for such things know how many times an offensive lineman opened a hole for a runner or held off the pass rush so the quarterback had time to find his receiver and throw. The offensive lineman doesn't read his name in the newspaper statistics. All he gets is praise from his coaches and teammates. Yet these unsung players, doing the roughest sort of job, must excel in teamwork to make stars of the backs and receivers. That this happens so regularly in our individualistic society is merely remarkable.

In baseball, the World Series participants get together to divide their share of the Series receipts among all who contributed to the team. At this point, individual performance has little meaning. Equal shares go to the biggest star and to the bench warmers and spot pitchers. High batting averages and pitching victories do not bring a bigger share. Indeed, teams have historically given partial shares to players who were with the team only part of the year. Perhaps they were traded away or hurt or sent down to the minors. Trainers, clubhouse managers, and others are also remembered.

We glorify individuals, pay them high salaries, and make them celebrities, yet we expect them to be team players. We demand teamwork, yet by lauding individual excellence, we make team play hard to achieve. Strange it surely is.

NEW YORK YANKEES

The Yankees have won thirty American League pennants and twenty World Series. Their celebrated "Murderer's Row," with Babe Ruth, won three pennants in a row in the 1920s. The "Bronx Bombers" won four World Series in a row from 1936 through 1939. Under Casey Stengel, the Yankees won five consecutive World Series from 1949 through 1953. They won five pennants in a row from 1960 through 1964. In the eighteen years from 1947 through 1964, the Yankees won fifteen pennants and ten World Series. No other team in the history of baseball has won five World Series in a row. Only one other team, the Oakland A's of 1972–74, have won as many as three in a row. After 1964 the Yankees went into a tailspin that lasted more than a decade. Then they began to have strong teams again, winning the pennant in 1976 and the World Series in 1977 and 1978.

A Matter of Character

> We had tremendous pride. We loved to win, thought
> we could win, and did win. We had pride in ourselves
> and in each other, in the whole team.
>
> Bill Dickey

Along with all those pennants and World Series triumphs,
the Yankees have another distinction. They are the only
team to have a hit Broadway musical named for them. In
Damn Yankees, a diehard, middle-aged Washington Senator
fan sells his soul to the devil, who transforms him into a
youthful superstar to lead the Senators to the pennant over
the hated Yankees.

The plot may have been good theater, but it wasn't too
realistic. During the Yankees' long domination of baseball,
there were superstars aplenty. Bob Feller of Cleveland, Ted
Williams in Boston, Stan Musial in St. Louis, Willie Mays
of the Giants, and Hank Aaron of the Braves come in-
stantly to mind. Yet the Yankees ground on, remorselessly,
inexorably, even inevitably to pennant after pennant. No
superstar could stop them for long—or even a whole team

of superstars. In the 1950s, the Cleveland Indians assembled what is acknowledged to be the finest pitching staff in the history of baseball—and pitching is said to be 90 per cent of the game. Bob Lemon, Early Wynn, and Mike Garcia were all 20-game winners. Bob Feller was a bit past his prime but still a consistent winner. The bullpen had Ray Narleski and Don Mossi as right-left relief men. Yet the Indians won only one pennant, in 1954. And they had to win 111 games to beat out the Yankees, who won 103, itself a Yankee record. Frustration was the cross borne by Yankee opponents for forty years.

What made the Yankees so great? The answer is surprisingly complex, for the Yankees were not one team over their long reign, but several teams. And those teams had radically different characters. The Bronx Bombers in the 1930s had little in common with the Yankees of the 1950s and 1960s. And neither of these teams is like the Yankees of today.

The Bronx Bombers were a classic Yankee team. Even today most people, when they think of the Yankees, think of that team. It may have been the greatest team ever assembled, dominating the American League from 1936 through 1943. Only World War II broke it up. The 1936 lineup reads like the Hall of Fame: Lou Gehrig on first, Tony Lazzeri on second, Frank Crosetti at short, Red Rolfe on third, George "Twinkletoes" Selkirk, Joe "The Yankee Clipper" DiMaggio, and Tommy "Old Reliable" Henrich in the outfield. Charley "King Kong" Keller later roamed there. Behind the plate was Bill Dickey catching a pitching staff that included Red Ruffing and Lefty Gomez. "Fireman" Johnny Murphy came in to douse any rallies by opponents.

There may have been four bases and three outs, but baseball was a much different game in those days. The ball was less lively, yet it was more of a hitter's game. Pitching wasn't so dominant. The hurlers threw basically a fast ball, curve, and changeup. The slider was not yet in use. There were relief pitchers, yet the modern practice of sending three or four strong-armed pitchers into a game was unthinkable in those days. A pitcher expected to go the full nine innings and considered himself a failure if the manager took him out. So the pitcher paced himself. He expected to give up hits and runs. In those days, a pitcher such as Feller or Ruffing was a star if he had an earned-run average of 3.00 over a season. Pitchers routinely gave up four and five runs per game and still expected to win.

There was a lot of hitting and scoring. The Yankees of that era could field a whole lineup of .300 hitters—especially when Ruffing was pitching. He was a good hitter and regularly pinch-hit for the team. Batting averages of .350 were common. An average of .375 or more was needed to win the batting title. Indeed, Ted Williams' .407 in 1941 was the last time a .400 hitter appeared in baseball. Batters expected to get 200 hits a season and knock in 100 runs. Dickey had 100 RBI seasons several years in a row and Gehrig regularly knocked in 150 or more runs a year. Today's .250 hitter probably wouldn't have made the majors in those days. A .280 hitter was considered a journeyman—if he hit the long ball and was a solid fielder. But again, it was a different game in those days.

I talked to Bill Dickey the day after his seventieth birthday. He was in fine health and had enjoyed the accolades that poured in on him the day before. And they were deserved. Bill Dickey, Hall of Famer, one of the great catchers and hitters of all time, manager, coach, and now a successful investment banker in Little Rock, Arkansas. And I talked to George Selkirk, now living in retirement in Florida. He, too, is in good health, playing golf regularly.

Dickey said of the Bronx Bombers, "We had everything—great hitting and superb pitching. And we had good defense. Lots of people forget that." Selkirk remembered: "In the ten years I was with the Yankees, it was very much a set team. There was no platooning. You were expected to hit all kinds of pitching. There were few changes. All of us would have done anything to avoid being traded from that team."

Two old men exaggerating the triumphs of their youth? Maybe, but not likely, for they were genuine triumphs. And they are important to understanding teamwork, for the Yankees of that era are still today a model for what a successful team tries to be.

The building of the Yankees as a team began with the selection of the players, a point that will be made repeatedly throughout this book. They all had great ability, certainly, but they were also of a certain type. Ed Barrow, then George Weiss, the celebrated Yankee general managers, looked for young men who were "gentlemen." Virtually to a man, the Yankee players were clean-cut, well-mannered, and respectful of authority. They were intelligent, serious, and studious, at least of baseball. Most came from poorer homes and hungered for the money, fame, and opportunity baseball could bring them. They were strong, quiet, and competitive. "I'm still competitive," said Dickey. "I love to win and hate to lose—even a game of checkers."

Players who didn't fit the mold were traded away, no matter how good they were. A famous trade of the thirties sent Johnny Allen, a fine pitcher, to Cleveland for Monte Pearson, who was considered not of the same caliber. Allen knew how to pitch, but he was a bit "flaky" by Yankee standards. Pearson fitted the mold and pitched well for the Yankees for several seasons.

Selkirk: "I never saw one serious incident of animosity

One of the great ones. Bill Dickey when he was behind the plate for the Yankees.

among the players. We had great respect for each other. We genuinely liked each other and our morale was tremendously high. We constantly encouraged each other. If one struck out, another said—or we knew—that someone would pick it up with a hit. There were no displays of temperament. Nobody broke up the locker room or dugout. It just wasn't done, and if you did it you wouldn't last long."

There was something more to this Yankee character. Dickey: "We had tremendous pride. We loved to win, thought we could win, and did win. We had pride in ourselves and in each other, in the whole team. But make no mistake. We played for money. None of us had much money and this was the only way we knew to get it. We wanted to win to get into the World Series. That World Series check meant a lot of money to us. That's all changed today. Reggie Jackson makes more in a single day than we earned from a whole World Series."

Another fact is important. Virtually to a man, those Yankees came up through the farm system. They had learned to be a Yankee in the minors and had gone through a harrowing competition to be a Yankee. They were not about to surrender their place in the Yankee lineup if they could help it. The Yankees were three and four deep in every position in those days. If a regular faltered, there were eager young guys ready to take his place.

Selkirk: "I read the papers every day to see how Henrich and Keller were doing down in Triple-A ball. If they had gone four for four, you better believe it made me try harder."

To recap, the Yankee team began with the selection of the players. All were of similar character and temperament. They had come up through the farm system. Being a Yankee was both the carrot and the stick. You played to make the team and you played to keep from being cast off it.

George "Twinkletoes" Selkirk, star outfielder of the thirties.

There was another ingredient to the Yankee success. The 1940 season illustrates it. The Yankees had won four straight pennants and would win again in 1941, 1942, and 1943. What went wrong in 1940? Dickey said, "We got off to a terrible start. Everything seemed to go wrong. When we finally got going it was too late to catch Detroit. We would have if the season had been a few games longer." Selkirk said, "I was hurt, Dickey was hurt. We just couldn't seem to get going."

There was another factor. Lou Gehrig, the "Iron Man," voluntarily stepped out of the Yankee lineup on April 30, 1939, after 2,130 straight games. It is considered one record unlikely ever to be broken. Gehrig soon learned he had a fatal illness. The once outstanding physical specimen withered visibly and he died on June 2, 1941. Dickey was his friend, roommate on the road, and bridge partner. He will not admit that the loss of Gehrig, not just as a player but also as a person, caused the poor 1940 season, but he does say he grieved for his friend, was extremely upset, and could think of little else. "I blamed myself for our failure, but I couldn't seem to do anything."

Gehrig was the team captain and team leader. What he meant to the Yankees cannot be measured. He was the model for the team, quiet, strong, outstanding in his ability, infinitely respected as a player and as a person. Selkirk: "We loved him. That's all there was to it. Everyone patterned himself after Lou: You never knew if he went 0 for 5 or 5 for 5. It didn't matter how much you hit or what your batting average was—as long as you did your part in a victory. There was never any bellyaching around Gehrig."

Dickey: "Gehrig was the greatest player who ever lived. No statistics can measure what he was to us. Oh statistics can show how many times he knocked in 150 or 175 runs a season, but statistics won't show how many of them came in the clutch. We always knew that if we got on base or if we failed to knock in the runs, Gehrig would do it for us. There has never been a clutch hitter like him. You don't know what it meant to know he was in the lineup."

In running his inconceivable stretch of consecutive games, Gehrig played hurt many, many times, yet never spoke of it, never complained. He was dubbed "a quiet hero." His simple presence in the dugout made the Yankees a team and made them try harder as a team.

In their great years, the Yankees always had a great leader. Gehrig was succeeded by Joe DiMaggio, another quiet man, counted on by his teammates to get the job done. He was the leader, the perfectionist, the one who tried hardest, the person who set the example for the others.

In his book *Dynasty: The New York Yankees 1949–1964,* Peter Golenbock quotes Yankee pitcher Ed Lopat concerning DiMaggio. It was a hot, humid day in Washington and the Yankees were playing a doubleheader. The Yankees won the first game; then Yogi Berra, a slugging young catcher, begged out of the second. With Berra's replacement going hitless, the game ground to a 3–3 tie, called because of darkness. After the game, DiMaggio, so tired he could barely stand, confronted Berra in the locker room. As Lopat remembered it, DiMaggio said, "What the hell's wrong with you?" Berra asked what he meant. DiMaggio said, "You're twenty-three years old and you can't catch a doubleheader?" Lopat said, "You could have heard a pin drop in that clubhouse. He chewed him out for twenty minutes." After that it was extremely difficult ever to get Berra out of the lineup. He insisted on catching doubleheaders.

DiMaggio's replacement as team leader was Mickey Mantle. Second baseman Bobby Richardson, Mantle's friend

Perhaps the single most loved and respected athlete the United States has ever had—Lou Gehrig.

and teammate in the 1950s and 1960s, speaks of him as men a generation before had of Gehrig. "Mickey was a real team leader. He was no chatter guy but he set the example in his own way. He was competitive as a player and as a person. He wanted only to win. He wasn't thinking of batting averages or records. He wasn't thinking of himself. He wanted only to help the team win."

Richardson says his greatest thrills in sports were provided by Mantle. "There were two of them. Twice Mantle had been out of the lineup because of injuries. When he returned and stepped into the on-deck circle, a tremendous roar went up from the crowd when they saw him. There was another huge roar when he stepped to the plate. On each occasion Mantle stroked a tremendous home run, showing he was back. I still get goosebumps thinking about it. He could rise to the occasion. He could do what had to be done. He was the leader."

Many coaches and players in so many sports speak of the importance of the team leader. It seems to be a key ingredient in the success of a team. The Yankees were so successful for so many years because they had a succession of outstanding leaders. It is no accident that the decline of the Yankees began with the loss of Mantle and the absence of a successor of his caliber.

In their heyday, the Yankees had owners who were intensely interested in the team—first "Jake" Rupert, then Dan Topping and Del Webb. These were sportsmen in the finest sense of the word. They wanted to win and they were prepared to do all that was required to win. Many have pointed out that the Yankees, as consistent winners, attracted such huge crowds to Yankee Stadium and every other city they played in that the team virtually manufactured money. No small part of the Yankee success was their status as the wealthiest team in baseball.

Only one word need be said: DiMaggio.

But Rupert, Topping, and Webb did not look upon the team as a purely money-making operation. They did not siphon off all the money into their pockets. Much of it was reinvested in winning. The Yankees had a peerless scouting system, picking up players wherever they could. The farm system was always stocked with promising players who were brought along as replacements for the Yankee lineup or as trades for established players. The Yankees were an organization from top to bottom, from the rawest rookie in the lowest league to the front office in New York. And the owners took a personal interest in all of it. They knew the Yankee players as individuals, not just as athletes. The Yankee character stemmed in no small way from the fact that the owners were "gentlemen" and wanted people of this caliber to play for them.

The owners also hired general managers of outstanding ability to run the day-to-day operations of the organization, negotiate player contracts, and arrange trades. The Yankees were fortunate in two longtime general managers, Ed Barrow and then George Weiss. Perhaps the best way to show the influence of these two men is by contrast with the brief tenure of Larry MacPhail, father of current American League President Lee MacPhail. The elder MacPhail is considered to have been an authentic genius. He built the Dodger farm system. He introduced night baseball. He made daring trades. He added excitement to an often dull game and attendance increased wherever he went. But MacPhail was highly individualistic and often flamboyant, a man much in the spotlight, frequently controversial—the antithesis of the organization man. He was part owner and Yankee general manager for about two seasons in the late 1940s. He won one pennant. The team was a good one. But there was dissension on the club and the sort of turmoil on which MacPhail seemed to thrive. The Yankees might

Bobby Richardson getting ready in spring training in 1963.

have remained winners under MacPhail, but the Yankees would have had a much different character than the old Yankee teams under Barrow. Topping and Webb replaced MacPhail with Weiss, who was less individualistic and a more conservative man. Another Yankee dynasty began.

The Yankee managers have been vital to the team's success. Joe McCarthy managed the Bronx Bombers. He is in the Hall of Fame as a manager, yet he remains less appreciated than he ought to be. It was always said of the Yankees of that era that the team was so good that anyone could have managed them. But that is a misreading of McCarthy's contribution. For starters, he was himself the model of the Yankee character. He was a gentleman and expected his players to be the same. A story is told of a more playful Yankee giving hotfoots to a couple of his teammates. McCarthy rebuked him sharply for what he considered childish conduct and soon traded him away.

McCarthy was a keen and constant student of the game and had the ability of total recall. Tommy Henrich tells the story of a club meeting to discuss the opposing players. McCarthy asked if anyone knew anything about a certain player. Henrich had played with him in the minors and knew he had trouble hitting a changeup. But Henrich didn't say anything. Then McCarthy remembered seeing the player in an exhibition game some years before. "It seems to me he had trouble hitting the changeup." Henrich knew then the player was in trouble and he indeed did hit poorly in the series.

McCarthy resigned early in the 1946 season. He had disagreements with MacPhail, and the tensions of his fifteen years of managing had taken their toll. Bill Dickey replaced him as manager for that season and expected to be renamed. Instead, MacPhail chose Bucky Harris, a seasoned veteran of the managerial wars. Harris won the pennant in

The late Joe McCarthy. As manager of the Bronx Bombers in the 1930s and 1940s, he made it look so easy that he seldom received the credit he deserved.

1947, after which MacPhail was bought out by Topping and Webb and dumped by the Yankees. Harris stayed on through 1948. The Yankees were in the thick of the pennant race till the very end. They were forced out by Boston, who then lost to Cleveland in a playoff game. The Yankees' third-place finish was used as an excuse to fire Harris. Actually, there were serious clashes between the conservative Weiss and the easygoing Harris. Weiss thought players should have curfew, be in bed, and be prepared for the next day's baseball. Harris thought a little nightlife and partying were simply good, clean fun. Harris got the ax.

His replacement for the 1949 season was a surprise— Casey Stengel. At fifty-eight he was not only considered old for the job, but both as a player and a manager he had a reputation as a clown. He had never managed a winner in the majors. With his garbled speech and run-on sentences he could seldom remember his own players' names, for example—he had a reputation as an inept if colorful manager.

Behind the garbled language and malapropisms lay a splendid baseball mind. He was a serious student of the game. It was his passion. He might have trouble remembering names, but he knew everything about his players and what they could do. Like McCarthy, he had total recall of everything concerning the game and those who played it. After five straight pennants and World Series victories, Stengel well deserved his nickname, "The Ol' Perfesser."

Stengel was unceremoniously dumped after the 1960 season (along with Weiss) as too old to manage. Stengel then went on to manage the New York Mets for several seasons. He never won a pennant there, but was hardly expected to win with the team of castoffs and rookies he had to manage. Stengel's successor with the Yankees was Ralph Houk. He had been groomed to be a Yankee manager and could

"The Ol' Perfesser," Manager Casey Stengel of the Yankees.

not be kept in the wings any longer. Finding a place for
Houk was the real reason Stengel was fired. Houk won
three pennants, then moved up to general manager. Yogi
Berra won the 1964 pennant, then was fired after losing the
World Series in seven games. That season marked the end
of the Yankee dynasty for at least ten years.

The teams that won fourteen pennants in sixteen years
under Stengel, Houk, and Berra were not classic Yankee
teams in the sense of the Bronx Bombers. To be sure, there
were great players on those Yankee teams: DiMaggio, then
Mantle, Roger Maris, and Yogi Berra behind the plate;
great pitchers such as Allie Reynolds, Vic Raschi, Eddie
Lopat, and Whitey Ford. In the infield there was the great
Phil Rizzuto at short. There were many other quite good
players, Hank Bauer and Gene Woodling in the outfield,
Jerry Coleman, Tony Kubeck, Billy Martin, Bobby Richardson, Clete Boyer, Andy Carey, Joe Collins, and Joe Pepitone in the infield.

The Yankees of those years were obviously good or they
wouldn't have won so often, but it wasn't a devastating roster of .300 hitters and overpowering pitchers. Cleveland
had a better pitching staff and so did the White Sox for
many years. The Red Sox often had more potent batters.
Indeed, the Yankees had persistent weaknesses at third and
first and at various times the outfield was not calculated to
strike terror into the hearts of opposing pitchers. Those
Yankee teams didn't dominate baseball as the Bronx
Bombers had. The New Yorkers often had to scramble hard
for victories.

In those sixteen years, the Yankees were never a set
team. On any given day the Yankee lineup was both a mys-
tery and a fascination. Stengel in particular liked to platoon
players: right-handed batters against left-handed pitching,
and vice versa. He substituted frequently and pinch-hit even

The Yankees always had a team leader: first Gehrig, then DiMaggio, then this fellow—Mickey Mantle.

more. He moved players around to various positions. It became the era of the utility player. And it became the time of the relief pitcher. At the first sign of trouble, Stengel brought in a fresh, strong arm. Games became longer. Baseball changed.

Stengel was accused of overmanaging. But no one could challenge his results. Where Joe McCarthy was denigrated for having such a good team anyone could have won with it, Casey Stengel began to be considered a genius. He did nothing to dispel that reputation.

Gene Woodling played a number of seasons under Casey Stengel, then was traded away. The Yankees of this period made a lot more trades than in previous days. Woodling had successful seasons for Cleveland and Baltimore. He continued to play till past age forty. He is today a successful cattle rancher in Medina County, Ohio. Woodling speaks almost in awe of Stengel, expressing the greatest possible admiration and respect for him. Yet the fights and quarrels between the two of them on the Yankees are legendary. Woodling hated being platooned and being taken out the game. He never ceased to tell Stengel what he thought of him. So great were their battles that even teammates were fooled. Richardson said in his interview, "There was only one player who didn't like Stengel—Woodling."

He was surprised when I told him of Woodling's affections for his former manager. And Stengel reciprocated it. At a clubhouse meeting Stengel said, "There's at least one guy on this team who I know won't talk behind my back." The whole team turned to look at Woodling.

Woodling tells this story: "When I was traded to Baltimore I couldn't seem to hit. The fans were disappointed in me and I felt I let everyone down. I was traded to Cleveland and I had good years there. I was lucky to be given a second chance in Baltimore and I was able to hit then.

Anyway, when I first went to Baltimore, Stengel came to town with the Yankees. Reporters asked him why I wasn't hitting for the Orioles. Stengel said, 'Oh they're just not making him mad enough.'"

Woodling says he admired Stengel for two things: his memory and his ability as a psychologist. Many of Stengel's managerial moves, his platooning and substituting, were pure psychology. Woodling: "He knew every player on the team and he knew how to get the most out of every one of them. He'd encourage one person, criticize another, give a fatherly pat on the back to one guy, frighten and intimidate others. But his favorite technique was to make you mad. He knew that was the way to get the most out of me. I'd be so mad I'd go out there on the field just to show him."

Richardson: "Stengel knew I wasn't the sort of fellow to play well under criticism or ridicule. But I remember one time he pinch-hit for me in the first inning. I was so mad not even to get a chance to bat. It was the supreme insult and I stormed back into the dugout. He told me to get my gloves and go out to the bullpen to catch the pitchers. I was mad at him, but I was also determined to show what I could do."

The stories of Stengel's managing are legion, his skill in handling his players, his ability to outpsych opponents and to take advantage of even the smallest weakness. He liked to pitch Allie Reynolds in the second game of double-headers when his fast ball would be hard to see coming from the bright sun of the mound into the shadows at the plate. One more: A big factor in the Cleveland pennant in 1948 was a rookie pitcher Gene Bearden. He won twenty games and pitched the playoff victory over the Red Sox. His only effective pitch was a tantalizing knuckleball, which fluttered toward the plate. Batters couldn't resist it and couldn't hit it. When Stengel became Yankee manager the next season,

Gene Woodling—one of the RA's.

he threatened to fine any player who swung at Bearden's knuckleball. He knew him from the minors and was aware he could seldom get his knuckleball over the plate. Bearden soon walked himself out of the league.

Even if all credit is given to Stengel's genius, his managing could not have produced such a skein of pennants. As Dal Maxvill, former star with the St. Louis Cardinals and Oakland A's, put it, "Stengel's psychology didn't work with the Mets. He may have made the players mad on the Mets, but it didn't work any wonders. The Yankees had the players; the Mets didn't."

Maybe, but Woodling has another view of the Yankee success. As he put it, "We were a bunch of RA's." In sports parlance those initials stand for "Red Ass" and it is an expression to mean the player is mad and a fighter. Woodling explains further: "I don't mean we were a bunch of roughnecks or brawlers. We were far from that. Nobody ever broke up the locker room or dugout in a rage. But we played with what might be called controlled anger. We hated to lose and we got mad when we did. The more we fell behind the madder we got. When the going got tough, we got tougher. And in a key game, when the chips were down, there was absolutely no way we were going to lose. The whole team was that way. Those were angry men out there on the field. They were out to win and nobody, but nobody, was going to cross them.

"Take Vic Raschi. Off the field he was one of the nicest, quietest, most gentlemanly people I knew. On the field, he was an RA. He pitched with a terrible anger. I remember once, Stengel decided Raschi was pitching too fast. He signaled to Berra, a fantastic RA himself, to go to the mound and slow down Raschi. Dutifully, Berra went about halfway to the mound, then thought better of it. Raschi was in a tough spot and in a rage. There was no way Berra was going to say one word to him. We were all like that. We played to win and got mad when we didn't. That's what made those Yankee teams so great. That's why so many guys seemed to play better in a Yankee uniform. You can't be a great team unless you're mad."

Following their 1964 pennant, the Yankees went into a decline, languishing among the also-rans for ten years. What crumbled the once-proud dynasty? It is a problem much analyzed. Many answers are offered. A frequent answer seems to be the drying up of the farm system. Topping and Webb were looking around to sell the Yankees and neglected the farms. The players of the early 1960s were not replaced with men of the same ability. The Yankees were never able to come up with a leader to replace Mantle.

Another reason often given is racism. Jackie Robinson broke the color barrier in 1947 with the Brooklyn Dodgers. Other teams moved quickly to find and develop black players. There was no short supply. Willie Mays, Hank Aaron, and scores of others followed. "I will never allow a black man to wear a Yankee uniform," Weiss once declared. And he didn't. The Yankees could have had Mays but he was the wrong color to be a Yankee. Belatedly the Yankees brought up Elston Howard. He became a star and a Yankee in the finest tradition. But racism kept the Yankees from mining a major pool of fresh talent for many years. Other teams surpassed them because they sought the best players, regardless of skin color.

With their home-grown talent in short supply, the Yankees began to seek players through trades. With a team largely composed of men who were not "true" Yankees, pride and teamwork declined. The Yankees became a team of individualists and there were not enough good ones of those.

Every ex-Yankee I spoke to (as well as most authors) believe the sale of the Yankees to the Columbia Broadcasting System encouraged the decline. What had been a sport became a business. The personal touch between owner and player was lost.

Something more subtle happened. Richardson remembers, "When I first came to the Yankees the team used to give shares of the World Series money to guys who had maybe only played a few games or been with the team for a short time. They'd remember clubhouse boys and oh lots of people. They gave me a third share my first year and I'd hardly contributed anything. I was touched. These guys were so generous I couldn't help but love and respect them. In my ten years with the Yankees I saw it go the other way. They began to cut guys out of the share. There was no sense of divvying up the winnings. It was everybody out for himself."

Everybody out for himself. There began to be dissension, backbiting of managers, quarrels among the players. None of this had existed before. In an interview, pitcher Jim Bouton described drinking and carousing among the players, as well as Yankees who were drunk while playing. He told of snickering and backbiting when Johnny Keane, who succeeded Berra as manager in 1965, tried to stop it. He told of hating Keane because he wanted the team to win in spring training and not just goof off in the Florida sun. It was enough to make a Gehrig or a DiMaggio, a Dickey or a Selkirk, a Rizzuto or a Lopat or a Woodling hang their heads in shame. The Yankee character was as gone as the winning seasons.

To rub salt in the wounds of the Yankee fans, CBS completed its organizational disasters by firing the popular Mel Allen, the "Voice of the Yankees." The fans stayed away in droves. And why not? The team was lousy. All the familiar faces were gone.

Then the Mets came to town. They hired the Yankee discards, George Weiss in the front office and Casey Stengel to manage. Yogi Berra was made a coach along with Gil Hodges, the popular Brooklyn Dodger. In the twilight of his career Willie Mays came back to New York as a Met. For years the Mets were a disaster on the field, but the fans loved them. And when the Mets won the pennant ("You gotta believe") in 1969, New Yorkers thought it was the Second Coming.

By 1975, the Yankees were back. They won the pennant in 1976 and the World Series in 1977 and 1978. What has caused the resurgence? The most significant factor seems to be a change in ownership. CBS wearied of the money-losing ball club and sold it to a group headed by George Steinbrenner. He is a sportsman and is taking a personal interest in the team. As Jim "Catfish" Hunter puts it, "I own dogs, and like every owner, I want the best dogs. Steinbrenner owns the Yankees and he wants the best players and the best team. He is taking a keen interest. I think he wants to own a championship team."

But the Yankees of today are different from the old Yankees. None came up from the farm system. "This team is made out of twenty-four teams," Hunter said. Steinbrenner, aided by experienced general manager Gabe Paul, spent lavishly for the best players he could buy, including Catfish Hunter. The Yankees are a collection of high-priced individual stars, the highest-priced being Reggie Jackson, the former Oakland slugger.

Still, the chemistry seems to be there to make a winning team. Hunter: "This team has only one real problem. The only way it doesn't fit together is there are guys sitting on the bench who played every day for other clubs. Maybe

Jim "Catfish" Hunter toils for the Yankees now, but perhaps his great years were with Charlie Finley and the Oakland A's during their championship years.

When everybody knows you by your first name and a candy bar is named for you, you've arrived. Reggie Jackson, star outfielder for the Oakland A's and now the New York Yankees.

they played every day for six or seven years. Now they're on the bench. They are confused by this and it creates a little dissension. Otherwise, this is a club that pulls together. We want to win and we think we will win."

"Big Pete" Sheehy, longtime clubhouse manager for the Yankees, recalls a perhaps salient fact. During their era of dominance, the Yankee players were friends. "They all lived near each other. Their wives and families got along. After 1964, when the Yankees went into a decline, the players tended to be more scattered in where they lived. Today, a lot of the players live near each other down in Jersey. They have a car pool to and from Yankee Stadium. I think that's important in our winning again."

The Yankees seem to have learned some other lessons. Former Yankee great Billy Martin, who earned his fame as a pugnacious team player and RA, is scheduled to return as Yankee manager in 1980. Yogi Berra and Elston Howard are coaching. Yankee Stadium has had a major facelifting. It would seem attention is being paid to the fans again. Who knows? The Yankees may be starting another dynasty.

BOSTON CELTICS

In the competitive cauldron of the National Basketball Association, the Boston Celtics have created a record unlikely ever to be equaled. In the twenty seasons beginning with their first championship in 1957, the Celtics have won fourteen times, including eight in a row, nine of ten, eleven of thirteen. They won again in 1974 and again in 1976. In a twenty-seven-year span from 1950, the Celtics finished out of the playoffs precisely twice. During those years, the Celtics have changed entire player rosters several times. They have changed coaches and owners. The Celtic dynasty has been all the more remarkable because, as the perennial winner, the team had the last choice in the draft of college players.

Their Thing in Boston

> There is no compromise between yourself and the effort
> you are willing to expend.
>
> Bob Cousy

It is April 1976. The baseball season is already started. Football coaches are deep into strategy sessions for their approaching season. The National Basketball Association is concluding its championship series between the Phoenix Suns and the Boston Celtics. These two teams have been playing basketball, perhaps the most physically demanding of all major sports, since the previous August. Players on both teams are physically exhausted. Tommy Heinsohn, former star Celtic forward and then the coach, recalls what happened in the sixth and final game of the series.

"We had won the first two games and they won the next two. We beat them in Boston, then flew to Phoenix determined to end the series. Not only were we exhausted from the long season, we also had the long flight to Arizona. We were suffering from jet lag. The game went into triple overtime and it became a test of willpower. Who wanted to win more? We didn't choose the easy way to win. We ran right at them. We ran and ran and ran, and in that triple overtime we ran away to an 87–80 victory. Our opponents wanted to conserve their energy. We didn't, and our willingness to run brought victory."

To the Celtics, running is the name of the game. Once or twice a contest, particularly in important ones, the Celtics will start to run. They sweep both backboards, controlling the ball, racing the length of the floor in fast break after fast break. They may run off ten of fifteen points in a row. It is as if opponents are just standing there watching them. It is awesome to behold, deadly to opponents, and the Celtic trademark.

Heinsohn calls it "Our thing, *cosa nostra*. Other teams have tried to do it. But they are not as willing to commit themselves, their bodies, their energy to this style of play. For us this style starts with the belief we can do it. In a way it just sort of happens. As a coach I can't really order it from the bench. It just happens among the players. They become fanatics and there is little opponents can do to stop it."

There are several names for this fanaticism. Heinsohn calls it the "system." Arnold "Red" Auerbach, longtime coach and general manager who developed and designed the style of play, speaks of a "philosophy." Bob Cousy, longtime Celtic guard and one of the great players the game has produced, speaks of a "killer instinct." As Cousy explains it: "The Celtic mystique is simply a desire to be first. The players all have the killer instinct. Their desire to win is not diluted by big money. They are not products of a spoiled childhood. The Celtic mystique is nothing other than good players who complement each other and all of whom have the killer instinct."

When you say Boston Celtics you are really saying Red

Auerbach. Howie McHugh, public-relations director for the team, has been with the club since 1946, longer even than Auerbach. He says of Auerbach, "He made the deals, drafted the players, ruled with an iron hand, established Celtic pride. He coached the team for sixteen years and has been the general manager since 1966. The Celtics *are* Red Auerbach."

Cousy again: "The Celtics are a product of the genius of Red Auerbach. His greatest ability is to be able to sustain the kind of effort, from himself as well as the players, for a longer period of time than any other team. His record of eight world championships in a row will never come close to being duplicated. It is one thing to motivate a team to win a championship. It is much more difficult to keep a team from letting down to win a second time and a third and a fifth and an eighth time. That Auerbach did it is incredible. I'll mortgage my home to bet that it will never be duplicated in any sport."

How did Auerbach accomplish this feat of motivation? Cousy's answer: "It's what I mean by the killer instinct. It's more than just a desire to win. It is a willingness to go all out, to do anything that is required to win. There is no compromise between yourself and the effort you are willing to expend. With killer instinct you will literally step on your own grandmother to win. You become capable of anything. To win year after year, especially in basketball, this is what you have to do. You have to want to win more badly and you have to hang in there longer than the competition."

What does Auerbach say of it? "I don't know how to express it other than a philosophical way of life. It is difficult to win and infinitely more difficult to win once you've won. The motivation factor becomes so difficult. Everybody is out to beat you. Everybody is doing their best against you. Yet we won eight years in a row. It was very difficult. The measure of that is the fact that in the last eight years no team has won twice in a row, including the Celtics."

In his interview with me, Auerbach was not very articulate about how he motivated the team. The best he could say was, "Oh there were so many ways. You're asking about ideas and thoughts and attitudes." Asked again for the secret to his motivation, Auerbach said, "We were in better physical shape than other teams. We worked harder. We were a very disciplined team. There were no petty jealousies. Other teams develop cliques among the players. We never had that. We had a lot of pride. We played together as a team for the benefit of the team."

Heinsohn, who was a star player for Auerbach and is now a veteran coach, is a bit more analytical of what it is the Celtics do. "It begins with the selection of the people who play for you," he said. "We try to pick people who have the temperament for our type of play. They may have fantastic ability, but if they aren't capable of the integrated teamwork required in championship basketball, if they don't have the unselfishness to surrender their own individuality for the good of the team, then they aren't going to make the Celtics. You can have five superb players and still not have a team."

Auerbach says of this point: "We'd sometimes get a kid who didn't fit in. We'd get rid of him. And we didn't make a lot of trades. I always thought it better to teach and develop our own players. I often thought we were better off with players with a little less ability that fit the mold we were working with."

If there are players who cannot fit into the Celtic concept of team play, then there are others who blossom under it. Heinsohn speaks of Charlie Scott, a recent Celtic star. "He had played for two other teams and was never on a winning one. I think the problem was that Charlie was asked to carry the whole burden of winning. If he had an off night, he felt like he was letting the whole team down. It is a tremendous thing to carry on your shoulders what should be arrived at collectively. When he came with us he fit in very well. He could contribute a great deal without scoring forty points a game. As a result he began to do things, like play defense, that lots of people hadn't known he could do."

What type of player makes a Celtic? A person who has the unselfishness to make a team player, certainly. A person with the killer instinct, to be sure. But there is a little more. His temperament blends with the others. The players genuinely like each other. They are, if not close friends, men who can spend hours a day in close proximity to each other and still play together on the court. Heinsohn: "Basketball is unlike football in a significant way. Football can be directed from above. There are set plays and there is a coach and quarterback who directs every thought. There is a huddle before every play. Only one guy has anything to do with strategy. Basketball is much more reactive. It is more integrated. There is constant motion. The player hasn't time to think and execute a strategy. He has to react to what others are doing. There has to be teamwork. Each player has to know the other extremely well."

In his autobiography, *Red Auerbach,* Auerbach gave another clue. He wrote that he expected his players to conduct themselves as gentlemen. If that sounds like the old New York Yankees, it is undoubtedly no accident. Auerbach said he expected nothing to occur in the player's private life that would interfere with his ability on the floor. That included drinking and enjoying the nightlife. Auerbach never hired a detective to watch his players or imposed a curfew. He simply expected his players to police themselves so they were in top shape for every game. Auer-

Bob Cousy in action against Syracuse.

bach was interested in the whole person, not just that part of him that played basketball. He tried to see that his men were well paid, had good living accommodations, put some of their money away for the future, and spent their off season preparing for the day when they were no longer able to play. He wanted extraneous worries eliminated as much as possible so they did not interfere with concentration upon winning.

The selection of players that fit together as a team, a Celtic team, was the ultimate genius of Auerbach. To appreciate the genius it is necessary to listen first to Cousy. "It is not very easy to find players for the NBA. There is a serious lack of talent. The ability to play at this level in the sport is so refined there just aren't enough players to go around. This year, out of all the colleges in the United States there is perhaps only one center with the ability to play in this league." NBA players compose a most refined and elite group of athletes. Not only is the talent pool small, but also, the Celtics have usually drafted last. Considering these obstacles, how did Auerbach form his dynasty?

It began in 1957. Cousy was already on the team, an established star since 1951. Heinsohn and Bill Russell were drafted in 1956, Sam Jones the next year, and K. C. Jones in 1958. They were the nucleus of the first great Celtic team. How did Auerbach get them? Heinsohn was a star at Holy Cross in Massachusetts. Auerbach got him with his territorial draft pick. In those days each NBA team could pick one player from its territory so a local boy could play on the local team.

Sam Jones came out of a small black school, North Carolina College. When Auerbach said his name at the draft meeting, others said, "Who's Sam Jones?" Auerbach had heard of him from Bones McKinney, then coach at Wake

Uneasy rides the champion, in this case Bob Cousy of the Boston Celtics.
(*United Press International Photo*)

Forest. K. C. Jones walked into Auerbach's lap. He had played with Bill Russell at San Francisco State and had been drafted as a football player by the Los Angeles Rams. Jones grew lonesome for his pal Russell, left Los Angeles, and joined the Celtics.

Auerbach admits he got lucky a few other times. In 1962, there was a bumper crop of big men from the colleges. Jerry Lucas, Bill McGill, Zelmo Beaty, Paul Hogue, Wayne Hightower, Leroy Ellis, Len Chappell, and Dave DeBusschere were all drafted before the Celtics picked. Auerbach chose a "little" six-five fellow who played under the shadow of Jerry Lucas at Ohio State. His name was John Havlicek. Another member of that Ohio State team, Larry Siegfried, walked into the Celtic camp because nobody drafted him. He contributed to the team for several seasons. Another player nobody wanted, Tom Sanders, became a star for the Celtics. Don Nelson, who filled the gap after the retirement of Heinsohn, had been drafted by Chicago, then sold to Los Angeles, where he couldn't make the team. He made the Celtics, all right.

It was the acquisition of Bill Russell that created the Celtic dynasty. The story of how Auerbach obtained him is now the stuff of legend. Everyone knew the San Francisco University star was a great one, and everyone also knew that Auerbach had no chance of getting him. The Celtics were drafting in seventh place and there was no way Russell would last that long in the draft. Also, there was a rule preventing teams from trading away their first-round draft picks, so Auerbach couldn't trade for him. Worse, the wealthy Harlem Globetrotters were interested in Russell for their exhibition tour.

Despite these obstacles, Auerbach tried anyway. He talked to Rochester, which had first draft pick. Rochester knew it couldn't sign Russell because the Globetrotters were offering too much money. They had decided to pass him up for a guard. St. Louis had the next selection. Auerbach offered to trade his popular center, Ed Macauley, for the right to select Russell. St. Louis also wanted another proven NBA player, Cliff Hagen. Auerbach swallowed hard. He was trading away a high-scoring, seven-time All-Star center and a sure-bet guard for an untried center who didn't score much. He agreed.

Next came the matter of the Globetrotters. Abe Saperstein, usually adept at such things, blew the negotiations for Russell. Instead of talking directly to Russell, Saperstein did all of his talking to Phil Woolpert, Russell's coach at San Francisco. Russell was offended. He felt like a piece of merchandise being bargained over and concluded there existed no amount of money that would make him turn himself into a clown on exhibition to play for the Globetrotters. Russell became a Celtic when the league owners changed the rule to allow the trading of first-round draft choices.

The rest is history. The Celtic dynasty began, and Russell revolutionized basketball. He couldn't score much, but he was fast and a defensive wizard, the stopper in the funnel. The guards and forwards forced the play toward the middle, where Russell, with his superb timing in blocking shots, barred the way to the basket. Russell didn't invent the blocked shot, but he made it an integral part of the game. His timing also made him a great rebounder, and his speed in getting the ball away to his teammates triggered the celebrated Celtic fast break. Russell played thirteen seasons and the Celtics won eleven championships. He has been retired since 1969, yet in 1977 Auerbach spoke of him as "simply the greatest player the game has ever known."

Howie McHugh suggests another story about Russell that he believes illustrates the genius of Auerbach. As the former coach tells it, Auerbach was exhausted after the 1966

Believe it or not, the Boston Celtics were winning, but you'd never know it from the expressions of Bill Russell, John Havlicek, and a disconsolate Red Auerbach, the coach, in this 1965 photo. The Celts were beating the Cincinnati Royals, 121–104, but this trio on the bench had just learned that the Philadelphia 76ers had defeated the Baltimore Bullets to win the Eastern Division championship. The Celtics were second and anything but used to that. But the Celtics went on to win the playoffs and the championship. (*Associated Press Photo*)

season and retired as coach. McHugh has another version: "Russell was also talking about retiring as a player. So Auerbach retired as coach and named Russell to succeed him. This kept Russell on as a player-coach. Russell wasn't much of a coach, but as a player we won two more championships with him."

Russell's retirement, both as player and coach following the 1969 season, was a seemingly irreplaceable loss to the team. The Celtics slid to sixth, then climbed back to third. Then the dynasty reasserted itself. Beginning in 1972, the Celtics made the division finals every year through 1977, winning the championship in 1974 and 1976. These "new" Celtics again have brought a new dimension to basketball. They still run and run, as the older teams. They still have peerless teamwork. But they lack the big man. When Auerbach drafted Dave Cowens in 1970 to replace Russell, many an eyebrow was raised. At six-eight, Cowens was considered too short to play with the seven-footers in the league. Most teams would use a six-eight at forward, not at center.

Heinsohn tells what happened. "After Russell retired, we began to use three centers, one of whom was Dave Cowens. We had one man who was fast, another who was fast and a good outside shooter to bring opposing centers away from the basket, and a big strong guy to muscle them under the basket. Ultimately, Cowens was able to do all three jobs. He is extremely fast and a good outside shooter, and he is strong enough to take the rough stuff under the basket. And he is a superb defensive player. Dave brings tremendous enthusiasm to the game and plays with great intensity. If we are up against the super big guy, we use quickness and mobility against him. If it is a challenge for Dave to play the super big men, it is just as much a challenge for them to play against his speed, outside shooting, and defensive abilities."

In building another winner around "little" Dave Cowens, the Celtics again showed their adaptability. In Cousy's terms, "A successful team must get the best players regardless of position, speed, or size, and they must blend together. It is an error to force the men to play a certain system. You have to mold the system to fit the physical abilities of the players you have." The Celtics used one system with Russell and another system with Cowens.

These are details of strategy, however. More important than strategy or the men to carry it out is Auerbach's "philosophy." As Heinsohn puts it, "Basketball is a simple game. Defense is everybody doing his job. Offense is just hustle."

So what is the philosophy? Heinsohn: "It is to go all out to make the other team pay the price to beat you. The more you move the ball and pass the ball, the more the philosophy works. It is most discouraging to play us. We are willing to go all out all the time to win. As I said, it is *cosa nostra,* our thing. Where other teams are pacing themselves, husbanding their strength, saving something for I don't know what, we are going all out to win. We try to run our opponents till they are tired. We try to play our bench against their bench. We try to get our better people against their weaker people or our better people against their tired better people. The game is forty-eight minutes long and we try to make them play all forty-eight minutes of it—as fast and as hard and as all-out as the game can be played."

There is something more that has made the Celtics such a great team. Perhaps it lies in a story Auerbach tells of a secret meeting the team had in 1965. The Celtics had won seven straight championships and were leading the league that season. But something was wrong. The team was playing .692 ball, but they had been playing over .800 ball the year before. Worse, they were dropping close games to good teams they used to beat. The savvy Celtic fans had even booed them. In that situation, the Celtics got together for a secret meeting—secret from Auerbach. They thrashed it all out, pointing out each other's mistakes and admitting their own. The consensus seemed to be that the team wasn't putting out as in previous years. On defense, guards and forwards were letting down, knowing Russell was always at the end of the funnel to block the shot. But Russell was no longer young. The spring had gone from his legs. His reflexes had slowed. He admitted he wasn't playing well, certainly not well enough to make up for the lapses of his teammates. The players even criticized Auerbach in absentia for not trying as hard as he had in the past. The criticism got back to Auerbach and he admitted it was true. The Celtics, including their coach, began to try harder.

It takes more than rap sessions and determination to win basketball games. It takes youth and speed, and the Celtics, having won seven championships in nine years, were no longer young. As the sportswriters put it, the nucleus of the Celtic team had lost a step to their opponents. The Celtics tried hard. They played .675 ball. But winning two thirds of their games got them only second place in the East. It was the first time they failed to win the division in a decade. Guts and desire and cosa nostra were not enough—or were they?

In the playoffs, the Celtics first met a strong Cincinnati team led by Oscar Robertson in a best-of-five series. The Royals beat the Celts on their home floor and the fans could begin to read the handwriting on the wall. The Celts traveled to Cincinnati and stormed back to a 132–125 triumph. The teams played again, each losing on their home floor. Finally, in the fifth game, at Boston Garden, the Celts put it away, 112–103.

Boston then met the Philadelphia Warriors in the division finals. Philadelphia, led by Wilt Chamberlain, who teamed with Hal Greer and Chet Walker, was a super team. They had beaten out the Celtics in regular-season play. Chamberlain was the most overpowering offensive player the game has ever known. Seven feet, two inches tall, weighing 265 pounds, he was a scoring machine. He had scored 100 points in a single game and averaged 50 points for a season. The scoring record book virtually needed a byline— "By Wilt Chamberlain." He was "Mr. Offense," and his battles against "Mr. Defense," Bill Russell, are legends. In this series it was all Russell, his hand blocking Chamberlain's shots, the two of them struggling for rebounds. The Celts demolished the Warriors in four out of five games.

The championship series was against Los Angeles. It was a splendid team, with Elgin Baylor, Jerry West, Gail Goodrich, and others. The Celtics were hurting. *Time* magazine wrote: "Boston guard K. C. Jones was wearing so much adhesive tape he looked like a Fourth Dynasty mummy." Sam Jones had water on the knees. Russell was wearing a huge bandage on his right leg. *Time* thought it looked like he was wearing long johns. The difference was John Havlicek. He was known in those days as the "best sixth man in basketball." He came off the bench to score 41 points against the Royals in two games. He scored 127 against Philadelphia in five.

Los Angeles won the first game. Boston won the next three. Then the Lakers, led by Jerry West, won the next two. The deciding game was played at Boston Garden. With Russell and Havlicek leading the way, the old men of Boston ran off a 10–0 lead in the first four minutes. In the third quarter they lead, 76–60. With 25 seconds left to play

"Out of my way, big boy." The Celtics' K. C. Jones seems to be saying that as he drives on No. 13, Wilt Chamberlain.

and his team ahead by 10 points, Auerbach lit up a long black stogie. The Celtic fans roared their approval. Auerbach had a ritual. He never smoked during a game. He never lit up until his team was sure of victory. At that Auerbach was almost premature. In the waning seconds the Lakers found the basket, but a Celtic stall brought a 95–94 victory. Eight championships in a row. Russell spoke for all after the game, "Of all the Celtic teams this is the shortest in ability and the longest on heart."

This was not, however, the Celtics' finest moment. Red Auerbach retired as coach, but remained as general manager. Russell succeeded him as coach, becoming the first black coach of a major sports team. The next season, the Celtics continued to struggle. They were 60–21 for a .741 percentage, but trailed the Warriors by eight games at the end of the season. Boston beat the New York Knicks in four games but ran into Chamberlain's revenge in the division finals. Chamberlain had done everything in his career but win the championship. Russell and the Celtics had stood in his way all those years. In 1967 Wilt was not to be denied. He personally outplayed Russell, as Boston lost to Philadelphia in five games. Chamberlain went on to lead his team to the coveted championship. Everyone was sure the long Celtic dynasty was over.

The next season, the Celtics won two thirds of their games, but they were still eight games behind the leader, Philadelphia. Russell and company beat Detroit in a six-game series in the semifinals and again met Philadelphia in the division finals. It seemed a repeat of the previous season. The Celtics won the first game, then dropped the next three, two of the losses coming at home. Age was surely taking its toll on the Celtics. Incredibly, the Celts reached back for some reserves of stamina and poise. They won the next three games, including the final in Philadelphia. The championship series, again against Los Angeles, went six games, with the Celtics winning it on the road. Unbelievably, the dynasty had reasserted itself.

After the final game, Jerry West made an observation about the Celtics that went a long way toward explaining the team's success. "There is something there, something special," he said. "For instance, twice tonight the ball went on the floor and Siegfried dove for it. He didn't just go for it hard, he *dove* for it. And they're all that way on the Celtics, and you can't teach that."

The comeback championship in 1968 was still not the Celtics' finest moment. To expect another championship was ridiculous. The team was truly old now. Sam Jones was thirty-six, the oldest player in the league. He announced it was to be his last season. Russell was thirty-five. The average age of Boston, rookies and all, was thirty-one. Jones missed twelve games with an injury. Russell spent a week in the hospital near the end of the season suffering from physical exhaustion.

The team played less than .500 ball for the last half of the season and came in fourth in the division standings. That was good enough for the team to enter the playoffs for the thirteenth year in a row. They beat Philadelphia in five games. Then they entered an outstanding series against the New York Knicks, which had come on as a powerhouse team eventually to be champions. The games were low-scoring, for both teams were defense-minded. The Celtics prevailed in six games. In five of those contests, Russell played the full forty-eight minutes without relief.

The championship series against the Lakers was a classic. The already super Los Angeles team had greatly improved with the awesome presence of Wilt Chamberlain at center. The Celtics had surely run out of miracles. The Lakers won the first two games at home. Boston won the third at home.

The fourth game, at Boston, was a defensive struggle. The score was 88–87 in favor of the Lakers with fifteen seconds remaining. And the Lakers had the ball. Em Bryant stole the inbound pass, gave the ball to Sam Jones, who shot—and missed. The Celtics got the rebound and called time with seven seconds to go. There was time for one shot. During the time-out, Russell took himself out of the game. He was a notoriously bad foul shooter. He wanted his best shots in the game in case a foul was called.

When play resumed, the inbound pass went to Sam Jones. He was now old and tired, but he had been one of the great scorers in the history of the game. He lost his footing as he set up for the shot. He was off balance as the ball left his hand. A bad shot. The Celtic bench groaned. The shot had no chance, and there was Chamberlain under the basket for the rebound. The ball hit the front rim of the basket. It bounded straight up, hit the back of the rim, bounded up again—then fell through the net for a Celtic victory. The players stared at the basket in disbelief that the shot had scored. Jerry West called the basket "the Lord's will."

The Celtics lost the next game away, then won the sixth, at home, 99–90. Defense was carrying the day. Havlicek scored 37, 43, and 34 points in the first three games. West was even better. He tallied 53, 41, 24, 40, and 37 points in the first five contests. The two giants, Russell and Chamberlain, both old and tired, did little but neutralize each other. In one game they scored only one point between them in an entire half. Observers felt it was a case of Russell against Chamberlain while the other four members of each team played basketball.

In the deciding game, at Los Angeles, the score see-sawed and was close at halftime. In the locker room Russell said, "Whatever we're going to do, win or lose, let's do it

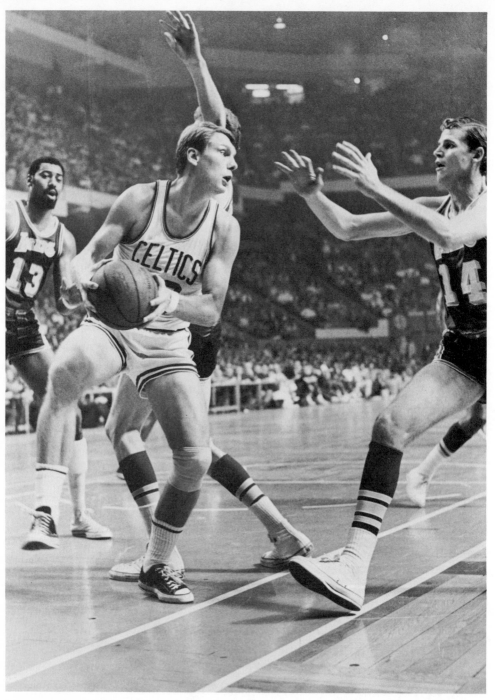

Trying to highstep out of a jam of Lakers (including No. 13, Wilt Chamberlain, and No. 14, Keith Erickson) is Don Nelson of the Boston Celtics.

together." The Celtics held off Los Angeles for a 108–106 victory, their finest moment.

After the game, Jerry West said, "It was as if we weren't supposed to win." Elgin Baylor, a superstar frustrated his whole career for a championship, said, "We had the home-court advantage. We had the personnel. We had everything." Everything but victory. Russell: "In other years we had more talent, but no team ever had more guts than this one."

The Celtics truly are remarkable. All those championships. Getting it up to win still another one when by all logic the team should have rested on its laurels, its players enjoying a happy retirement. There is surely something in the Celtics cosa nostra, their willingness to go all out to win and to force the opponents to play all out for forty-eight minutes if they are to beat them. Clearly, this "philosophy," as Auerbach calls it, is a secret to a championship team. Give no quarter. Never spare yourself for victory.

There was something else. In the last game of the 1969 championship series, Havlicek fell to the floor, apparently hurt. Russell rushed to him, put his arm around him, and led him off the floor. Asked later about the incident, Russell said, "I was thinking only that he might be hurt badly. You see, first, these men are my friends. Above all, we are friends."

BALTIMORE COLTS

No task was more difficult in this book than the selection of the teams to represent the National Football League— difficult because there were so many excellent choices. A few words of explanation are in order in hopes of assuaging the injured feelings of those many fans whose favorite team was not selected.

Remember the criteria. The team is to be dynastic, fielding strong teams over many seasons despite changes in personnel, coaches, even owners. I also wanted teams that were currently strong. And geography was a factor. No area could be represented by more than one team.

There were a couple of football dynasties in years gone by. The Chicago Bears come quickly to mind, as well as the New York Giants of the 1950s and 1960s. But both teams have fallen on hard times in recent years. I also passed up three super teams, the Green Bay Packers, Miami Dolphins, and Pittsburgh Steelers. Among them they have dominated the Super Bowl. I did not choose any of these teams because each were or are basically one team, one set of players who came together, flowered, and dominated their era. These three teams either have not or have not yet had the time to show the dynastic qualities of being great despite changes in players and coaches. I believe the same statement applies to two other NFL powerhouses, the Minnesota Vikings and the Oakland Raiders.

Perhaps the two teams in the NFL that most fulfill the criteria are the Los Angeles Rams and the Cleveland Browns. They were super teams for many years—the Rams still are—despite changes in personnel, coaches, even owners. I did not choose Cleveland in part because they are not now a contender and also because I was using another Ohio sports team. Los Angeles was done in by pure geography.

All these eliminations left two other teams in the NFL that can be called dynastic. The Baltimore Colts fielded a powerful team in the late 1950s, winning the NFL championship in 1958 and 1959. They again put together a super team in the 1960s, winning everything in sight, including the Super Bowl in 1970. They have a new and powerful team, making the playoffs the past two years.

The Colts have something else. They have been nurtured not so much on victory as on frustration. Theirs is an inspirational story of what teamwork can accomplish and what it means to be a team.

The Importance of Leadership

We had the greatest respect for him, the greatest love.
If he asked us to do anything, that's what we'd do.
                                                    Jim Parker

By reputation the "greatest game ever played" was the NFL
championship between the New York Giants and the Baltimore Colts in 1958. These two great teams played to a
17–17 tie then went into a "sudden death" overtime. The
Colts won it after eight minutes of play when a young John
Unitas threw pass after pass to Raymond Berry, setting up
a touchdown by Alan Ameche. It is a memory dear to the
hearts of football fans, particularly if they come from Mary-
land.

There have been many, many great games since then, including several "sudden death" endings. To single out that
particular game as the "greatest" is to enter a hopeless argument.

Nor was it in my opinion the greatest game the Colts
ever played. Many may disagree, but I would argue for an-

other game, played on December 26, 1965. To set the stage, after the Colts won their second championship in 1959, they went into a decline, chalking up mediocre records for the next four years. Those were years when the great Green Bay burst upon the scene and Baltimore, while good, was far from good enough.

It was different in 1964. The Colts swept to a 12–2 record for the Western Conference title, then rolled over and played dead in the championship game against Cleveland, losing, 27–0. The next year, Baltimore and Green Bay played out the season with identical 10–3–1 records. Two of the Colt losses were against Green Bay. Tied, the two teams met a third time in a playoff to determine the Western Conference championship. For Baltimore, a victory meant a return match with Cleveland, which had repeated as Eastern Conference champs.

It was a sorely wounded team that took the field that bitter cold day after Christmas in Green Bay. Johnny Unitas was hurt and could not play. His backup at quarterback, the talented Gary Cuozzo, was also injured and out. The Colts were a team without an experienced quarterback. They were forced to use Tom Matte, who had never played the position in the pros. He had been a quarterback at Ohio State, but a running quarterback, not a passer, and the Colts were a passing team. Matte undertook a cram course in the Colt playbook, but he still had the play information written on a wrist band. That piece of fabric is now in the Professional Football Hall of Fame at Canton, Ohio.

As Dick Szymanski, longtime Colt center and linebacker and now Colt general manager, recalls it, "We knew we weren't going to score much. We had to keep them from scoring." The result was an epic defensive struggle, with two superb defensive teams putting on a show of rugged hitting and fundamental football.

Johnny Unitas in action with the Baltimore Colts. Many consider him the greatest pocket quarterback of all time.

The Colt defense scored the team's only touchdown. With the game only twenty-one seconds old, linebacker Don Shinnick scooped up a Green Bay fumble and scored. The Colts managed a field goal shortly thereafter and had a ten-point lead. Could the defense hold? The defense played its heart out that day, as Green Bay ran eighty plays from scrimmage to the Colts' fifty-nine. Green Bay was held to one touchdown; then with a little over a minute remaining, Don Chandler kicked a tying field goal. Green Bay won it in "sudden death" with another Chandler field goal. It was a heartbreaking 13–10 loss for the Colts.

The next day the world discovered just how heartbreaking the loss was. The Baltimore newspapers ran on page 1 frame-by-frame photos, taken from the official game movies, of Chandler's game-tying field goal. The photos clearly show the ball going wide of the goal posts. More telling were the reactions of the players on the field. Chandler is seen kicking his foot in disgust, the Green Bay players turning away in dejection. The Colts are shown leaping for joy that Chandler missed. The last photo shows the official signaling the kick was good. Later, the goal posts would be extended upward and an official placed underneath to prevent just this sort of tragic error, but all this came too late to save the Colts that season.

Szymanski has another recollection of the game. "It wasn't just the disputed field goal. Late in the game when the Packers were driving on us, they were aided by two penalty calls. The calls were legitimate, no doubt of that, but officials hadn't been calling the infraction all season. Every team in the league had been guilty. It seemed a strange time to begin calling the penalty."

To me that game was the Colts' finest hour. They lost, to be sure, and to a superb opponent. After the game Coach Don Shula made no excuses. He could have suggested a

Colt General Manager Dick Szymanski when he was an All-Pro center for Baltimore.

different result had the Colts had a regular quarterback. Instead he said, "When you play a team three times in a season and fail to win, you don't deserve the title." But in defeat the memory of the effort made by the Colt defensive team lingers on as a source of pride to all football fans.

There is another view, offered by Bob Vogel, a six-time All-Pro offensive tackle for the Colts. He says, "Football is a game of emotion. I don't believe it is unusual for a team to get it up for a single game. But when you do it for an entire season, as the Colts did, that is something else."

To understand the 1970 season, which Vogel refers to, it is necessary to understand the Colt frustration that led up to it. The Colts were second to Green Bay because of the disputed field goal in 1965. They were second to Green Bay the next year. In 1967 the Colts produced a fantastic 11-1-2 season, but were again denied a conference title because Los Angeles had a similar record and the one game the Colts lost was to the Rams—on the last day of the season.

In 1968, the Colts compiled a 13-1 record and swept the playoffs to enter the Super Bowl highly favored over Joe Namath and the New York Jets. The Jet coach was Weeb Ewbank, who had coached Baltimore to their initial titles in the 1950s. The Jets pulled off a classic upset, 16-7. In the first half the Colts pushed the Jets all over the field, but couldn't score. The Jets scored, then held off the Colts' frantic attack. It was a bitter, humiliating loss for the Colts.

In 1969, the Colts did poorly with an 8-5-1 record and were second in the Coastal Division. Then came 1970, and Vogel recalls what happened. "We all felt we had been so close so many times. We all knew that if this team was ever to go all the way and become Super Bowl champs, this was our last chance. The team was getting old. It was this year or never. The simple fact was that we were far from the

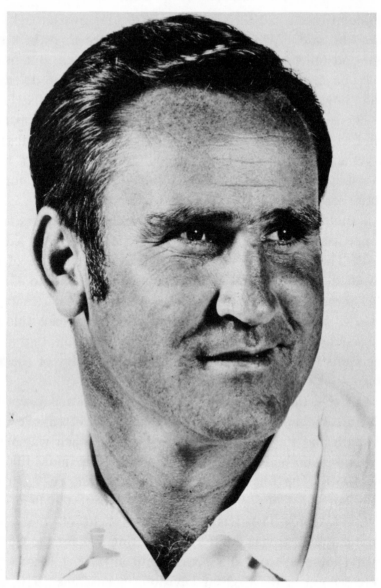

The winningest coach in professional football, Don Shula of the Baltimore Colts and the Miami Dolphins.

best team in the NFL that year. Yet Sunday after Sunday, game after game, we got ourselves up to win. Guys played their hearts out against superior opponents. It was something to see. I'll remember it all my life." For the record, the Colts went 11–2–1 over the season, and beat Cincinnati and Oakland to reach the Super Bowl against Dallas. It was a wild, untidy game, but the Colts prevailed on a last-minute field goal, 16–13.

The Colt record is truly outstanding. From 1957 through 1971, the team never had a losing season. The closest came in 1960 and 1962, when they lost as many games as they won. As we have seen, many of the other Colt teams were extremely strong, even champions.

To remain a strong team over a period of fourteen years in the NFL is an amazing accomplishment. Consider the obstacles. In that period of time, the personnel of the team must change, frequently several times, because of injuries, retirements, and trades. A consistently good team ranks low in the draft of college players. This makes it difficult to recruit the good young talent needed to maintain the championship status.

At the same time, the really good teams must be experienced. The men need to have played together both on offense and defense long enough to be a co-ordinated unit. Modern football is a brainy game. The physical talent is so nearly equal that the difference between winning and losing is often how consistently plays are run, the absence of mistakes, the correct reading of what an opponent is going to do, and the execution of a series of minor, virtually reflex adjustments while a play is in progress. Football players are often in a position of reading each other's minds during the few seconds a play is in progress. They need to know each other well and to have practiced and played together over a long period of time. Yet the frequent injuries and the draft

The face of Bob Vogel, former offensive lineman for the Baltimore Colts, mirrors the fatigue, concentration, and emotion that the sport of football demands.

make this difficult. For the Colts to have been so good for so long is a major achievement in professional football.

How were the Colts able to do it? Over that fourteen-year span there were two constants: Carroll Rosenbloom, the principal owner of the team, and Johnny Unitas, the quarterback. Colt players speak of Rosenbloom with the greatest respect. A typical statement comes from Bob Vogel:

"Carroll Rosenbloom was important to the Colts' success. He was a strong owner in terms of what happened to the team. He was physically there. He was not an absentee owner. And he offered a lot of warmth and love. I remember when my father was dying of cancer. Rosenbloom came to me and offered to arrange the best medical care possible. 'I'll fly him wherever you want him to go for treatment,' he said. I submit that went beyond the call of duty.

"Rosenbloom was a successful businessman. He understood that you need people and equipment to make a good business. And he understood that professional football is 90 per cent emotion. If you have a happy guy, he can perform miracles. An unhappy guy is not going to be a consistent player. Rosenbloom understood people. I know of no situation in which his business interests overran his sense of the importance of the player. But he could be tough. He wanted to win, and winning was all he understood. You never played games with him. He was so generous himself that if a player tried to take advantage of him, he was not long with the team."

Jim Parker, a Colt All-Pro and Football Hall of Famer, recalls being unhappy when he first came to the Colts. "The pros are different than college. At Ohio State we had nothing but the best equipment. Even our shoes were shined for us. When I went to the Colts, I found we had to make do with the equipment available. You had to make the team

Club owners, as well as players and coaches, make a winning team. One of the great ones is Carroll Rosenbloom, longtime owner of the Baltimore Colts, now principal owner of the Los Angeles Rams.

before they ordered equipment to size. So I ended up with a helmet that was too big. After four days I had a cut on my head. I spoke to Rosenbloom. He immediately ordered me three custom-made helmets. If you ever had any problems or needed anything, you knew you could count on Rosenbloom."

The great years of the Colts also coincided with the career of Johnny Unitas. He is ranked one of the best quarterbacks of all time, if not the greatest. He is frequently called the best "pocket" quarterback in history, meaning he seldom scrambled like a Fran Tarkenton, but dropped back and set up to pass from a protective pocket formed by his linemen and backs.

Perhaps the highest praise for Unitas came in an interview with the late Dan Reeves, longtime owner of the Los Angeles Rams. Reeves is in the Hall of Fame. He brought big-league professional sports to the West Coast, and he pioneered the scouting system now used throughout the NFL. Reeves said, "Unitas is the greatest quarterback ever to play the game. We had him and let him go. We still have the scouting reports on him. It's all there. It was all predicted. We just didn't keep him. He's the one player I regret the most letting go." It must be remembered that under Reeves the Rams had two fantastic quarterbacks named Bob Waterfield and Norm van Brocklin.

Reeves' scouts had seen Unitas quarterbacking for the University of Louisville, hardly a football power. The Rams drafted Unitas. They already had Norm van Brocklin, so they dealt Johnny to Pittsburgh. After a brief tryout, Unitas was cut. The future super quarterback began to play semi-pro ball. As Unitas recalls the story:

"After the Steelers released me, I received a telegram from Paul Brown, who was coaching the Cleveland Browns at that time. I talked with him by phone and he explained his situation. Otto Graham had retired and Cleveland wasn't too happy with its quarterbacks. But Brown talked Graham into coming out of retirement for one more season. Brown wanted me to sit out that season and sign with them the next. I said I would. I sat out the 1954 season. Then Weeb Ewbank, who was coaching Baltimore, called. He needed a quarterback badly and asked me to come. I told him about my conversation with Paul Brown, but the Colts sent me a contract for a thousand dollars. It was a bird in hand so I signed it and came to Baltimore."

In the telling and retelling of this tale, the thousand-dollar contract is usually ignored. In Baltimore, Unitas was obtained for the price of a sixty-five-cent phone call to Pittsburgh.

Unitas said of himself near the end of his career: "There are lots of men who are better passers than I, and, heaven knows, there are many who run better. I think there are better ball handlers, too, many of them. My greatest ability lies in knowledge of defenses, recognition of defenses in a game, and in making adjustments to offset defenses."

It is a strange statement. Unitas passed for more than thirty thousand yards in his career. He passed for more than three hundred yards twenty-one times. He held the record for most touchdown passes, most completed passes, and most consecutive games (forty-seven) with a touchdown pass. Yet he says his greatest ability was as a strategist. He studied game movies by the hour and learned to spot minis-cule signals—how a linebacker plants his feet, for example —which tipped off the defensive tactics. In a game he could check off his play called in the huddle and run a new one calculated to thwart the defense.

Unitas was a team leader par excellence. He was some-thing more than self-confident. At least when it came to football, he conveyed to his teammates a sense of total security about what he was doing. Whether the play worked or not, he had no shred of doubt that it was the right play.

Dick Szymanski, who centered the ball for Unitas many years, says: "A team of championship caliber must have a leader, and that leader on offense must be the quarterback. He calls the plays. When the going got tough, Unitas put the burden on himself. Before Unitas, in a third-and-one situation, the quarterback would send the fullback into the line. Unitas wouldn't ask anyone to do what he was not prepared to do himself. Third and one, he'd call a pass— put the burden on himself. That's standard now. Everybody does it. It was Unitas who began it."

Indeed, Unitas became known to Colt fans as the "Mississippi Gambler" because of the number of times he threw the bomb on third and short yardage.

Szymanski again: "When Unitas called the plays, you knew he had studied the other team. You had total confidence in that play. If you don't have that confidence, you get beat. It's as simple as that."

Jim Parker spent much of his career fending off defensive tackles and linebackers trying to sack Unitas. He says of Unitas: "In the huddle with John, you never said anything. You just listened. We had the greatest respect for him, the greatest love. If he asked us to do anything, that's what we'd do. If he said to kill somebody, that's what we'd do. It was that simple. I'd break my arm for him, both my arms, rather than let somebody hurt him. Look, if he breaks his arm, nobody eats. If I break my arm, everybody still eats."

Parker said that when any other quarterback came into the game it wasn't the same. "He didn't have control of the team. He didn't have the respect we gave Unitas."

How did Unitas earn that respect? Szymanski: "He worked harder than anyone else. We used to have to send an assistant equipment manager down to the practice field to get Unitas and Berry off the field so we could close up and go home." Unitas to Berry, the longtime Colt split end, was one of the celebrated passing combinations in football history. Parker: "John worked at football seven days a week. He ate and slept it. And everybody knew he knew what he was doing." Then respect, too, came from experience. Over the years, Unitas had completed so many last-second, game-saving passes that total confidence came to be deposited with him.

There were other ingredients than Rosenbloom and Unitas in the Colts' success. Rosenbloom picked great coaches. The first was Weeb Ewbank. He won two championships in Baltimore, then led the New York Jets to the upset victory in the Super Bowl over the Colts. Ewbank was followed by Don Shula. He coached the Colts in their heyday, then went to Miami, where he made the Dolphins into a super team.

Parker on Shula: "He is a football scholar. He is the smartest coach who ever lived. He simply knows more about football than anyone who ever coached the game." Vogel: "Shula has very strong organizational ability and he has been called a genius at the game, understanding both offense and defense. He is also sensitive to other people's needs, and people respond to that. He put together a good coaching staff that was capable and an extension of himself." Shula was followed by one of his assistants, Don McCafferty, who made the team Super Bowl champs.

Vogel: "I think there are several ingredients that make a team dynastic. You need the players, the coaching, the owner, the quarterback, the winning tradition. If you have two or three of these ingredients, you can have a good team. You must have all of them to be a great team. Take one ingredient out of this mix and the whole thing tends to fall apart. I think the Colts had one other ingredient that was most vital of all. Beginning in 1962, there was a very strong Christian influence on the Colts. It began with Don Shinnick, Jerry Logan, Raymond Berry, and myself. We were the first team to have regular Bible study and team chapel services. It gave us the maturity and love for each other to hang together in adversity. It caused many of the veteran players to pay attention to the rookies and help them along for the benefit of the team."

Parker: "I was one of the few people who knew that John Unitas went to church every day."

Szymanski: "Don't misunderstand, but I don't think prayer is going to win any games unless you have a good football team that pulls together. And don't kid yourself. You can't expect to make forty-five or fifty guys one big happy family. There will always be a certain percentage who don't get along. But the nucleus of the Colts were friendly and their families were friendly. That nucleus brought the others along and caused all to pull together as a team."

Those feelings, those ingredients that made the Colts a dynasty quickly fell apart. After their Super Bowl win in 1970, the Colts had another good season in 1971, with a 10–5 record. They entered the playoffs as a wild-card selection, beat Cleveland, then lost to Miami, which went on to the first of its Super Bowl appearances. The Colts' decline began in earnest after that. A 5–9 season was followed by a 4–10 season, and then, in 1974, a ghastly 2–11 season. This was a time of trial for the Colts. Carroll Rosenbloom sold the team to a group headed by Robert Irsay and took over the Los Angeles Rams. Irsay brought in Joe Thomas as general manager. His credentials were impeccable. He had built the powerhouse teams at Minnesota and Miami where he hired away Shula to lead the Dolphins to their impressive string of victories.

The only coach ever to win championships in two leagues, Weeb Ewbank. He coached the Baltimore Colts to titles in 1957 and 1958, then took the New York Jets to the celebrated upset victory over the Colts in Super Bowl III. (*Photo by George Hoxie, F.P.S.A.*)

In a series of moves that shook professional football to its core, Thomas literally cleaned house at Baltimore. He changed coaches. He traded Unitas to San Diego. One by one, sometimes in bunches, the old Colt players were traded away, sold, or retired. Not only were the older players eliminated, but virtually all the young, talented Colts, too. Many starred on other teams. It was as if the Colts were a farm club stocking the league.

The result was traumatic for Baltimore. Anyone associated with the old Colts went by the boards. It was as if all sentiment and nostalgia for the glory days had to be exorcised to make way for a new breed of Colt. It seemed a disaster. The Colts were a collection of also-rans nobody had ever heard of. In that dismal 1974 season, worse even than the 1953 and 1954 seasons when the Colts were an expansion team, Joe Thomas himself coached eleven games.

The improvement was as radical as the decline. By 1975 the Colts were back as division champs and into the playoffs. They made the playoffs in 1976 and were considered a threat for the Super Bowl at the start of the 1977 season.

The chief instrument for the metamorphosis is a brilliant young quarterback named Bert Jones. If he hasn't made the Colt fans forget Unitas, he has at least brought them to their feet cheering. Jones is himself dynastic. His father was an excellent NFL running back, Dub Jones. Bert was a consensus All-American at Louisiana State University in 1973 and a first-round draft pick by the Colts. He has matured into one of the best passers and playmakers in the league. His boss, general manager Szymanski, speaks of him as a team leader in the same way Unitas was. "In fact, one of the reasons Unitas was dealt away was the fact Bert Jones was waiting in the wings."

Two views of one of the great young quarterbacks in the NFL today—Bert Jones of the Colts. Sometimes it's harder on the sidelines.

Ted Marchibroda, head coach of the Baltimore Colts, is a study in concentration on the sidelines.

Jones speaks with pride of the club he leads. "The old Colts were just that, a little too old. Their day had come and passed. It became a case of sweeping the old away and bringing in the new. A lot of people knocked Joe Thomas for what he did. I'll admit I'm not sure there had to be such a quick sellout at that point in time. But there is no way to knock the ability of Joe Thomas and the things he did. He revamped an entire team from the ground up. And he did this far better than anyone else. Never has the nucleus of a good ball club been put together in such a short time."

Asked again about the wisdom of the sellout, Jones replied, "Who's to say who was right or wrong?"

To cast one man's opinion upon the waters of controversy, the radical surgery Joe Thomas executed on the Colts was not only necessary but also a stroke of courage and genius. The Colts were a tightly knit group, almost a family. The respect—one is tempted to speak of reverence —for Rosenbloom and Unitas created a situation in which comparisons were inevitable for any who followed them. There was no way, for example, that Bert Jones could earn the respect the older Colts gave Unitas. Jones would always be new, young, an upstart, replacing the master. There may have been other ways to do it, but in hindsight one very good way was to get rid of all who had played with Unitas, all who had known the tender regard of Rosenbloom, all who had been part of the Colt tradition.

As evidence, consider a statement made by Jones. "Football has changed a great deal since Unitas was in his prime. John didn't face the zones and different defensive strategies we have now." This indicates a laudable self-confidence in a young quarterback, but it is hard to imagine him saying that in front of veteran players who had known and respected Unitas. It would earn a comment such as, "You pip-squeak. Unitas was reading defenses when you were in diapers." Clearly, the old, all of it, had to go to make way for the new.

The new is pretty good. Jones: "I'm the team leader. I call my own plays. I stress the ability to play well consistently. I believe winning cures all. We all know what sacrifices it takes to win. There is no doubt we have the ability to win. And we are going to win. We are a team and we are all pulling together."

Jones also spoke on the question of high salaries being paid to athletes today. "Since the beginning of professional sports, everybody has tried to make as much money as they could. Everybody in every walk of life wants a higher salary. Being high-paid does not make a person less a player. Money is great, but when I get on the field, I think about winning and doing the best I can."

The Colts were down. There were a few bad seasons, as happened a couple of times in their history. Clearly the Colts are back. The dynasty on the Chesapeake is alive and functioning.

UCLA BRUINS

Question: What is the most remarkable, least likely to be equaled team record in the history of sports? This is a question calculated to bring on the sort of argument beloved by sports fans. A strong case can be made for the Yankees and Montreal Canadiens, winners of five championships in a row. It is a brave person who challenges the Boston Celtics' eight championships in a row, ten in eleven years.

I will argue, however, that the most awesome team sports achievement is the seven consecutive NCAA basketball championships won by the UCLA (University of California at Los Angeles) Bruins. Those seven in a row were part of ten the Bruins won in twelve years.

This is a mind-boggling record. There is a cardinal difference between professional and amateur sports. A professional team can play together for as many as ten or twelve years. Outstanding individuals can play baseball for twenty years. Many professional football and hockey players have had fifteen outstanding years.

By nature, colleges have a player only three years, four

at the most. To win seven national championships means UCLA had at least two great teams. Actually, it was three. To win ten or twelve means four or five superb teams, one after the other.

A Certain Selflessness

> It is the willingness of every guy to sacrifice his indi-
> viduality, his ego to the goal of winning as a team.
>
> Larry Farmer

From 1954 through 1975, UCLA dominated college basketball as few teams have ever dominated any sport. They
were the team to beat. They set team records unlikely ever
to be broken, including a tremendous run of eighty-eight
consecutive victories over three seasons.

They were playing the toughest sort of schedule. Two
and three times a week, at home and away, they met the
best teams in the land, and there are scores of superlative
college basketball teams. At the end of the season, the best
of these teams play off against each other in the NCAA
series to determine the one team that is best. Results are
based on a single game, win or lose. The championship
is not won in a best-of-seven series, as in baseball, hockey,
or professional basketball. A key injury, an off night by
a star player, or a lackluster performance can eliminate a
very good team in a single game. To put together the

teams and to overcome all the obstacles seven years in a row is merely incredible. And it must be remembered that these are college players. They have to study and maintain a grade average to play. Theirs is not a full-time job, as with professionals.

The UCLA dynasty began in 1964, and in many ways it was the most interesting of all the great Bruin teams. That team revolutionized basketball. The style of play they used is common today, but the simple fact is that it all began with that remarkable quintet of Walt Hazzard, Gail Goodrich, Keith Erickson, Jack Hirsch, and Fred Slaughter. On the bench were Kenny Washington and Doug McIntosh. As basketball players go—or grow—they were midgets. Slaughter was the tallest at center, six-five. Lots of teams had guards that big. Hazzard, the star and one of the great players of all time, was six-two. The team average was six-three. Many high-school teams were bigger.

So how did this miniscule team win the national championship—twice? The process began late in the 1963 season. It was essentially the same team and it had done well, winning the Pacific Coast Conference title, then losing 93–79 to Arizona State in the NCAA regionals. In the last few games of that season, the Bruins had begun to use a full-court press. A press is close guarding of opponents, and full-court means just that, all over the court. From the moment an opponent gets the ball, he is harried by a UCLA player. The idea is to make it hard for the opponents, particularly the guards, to bring the ball up the court. The press is supposed to force errors and turnovers and opportunities to score. There was nothing novel about the press. Most teams had used the full-court press from time to time, usually near the end of a close game in an attempt to get the ball. What was novel in that 1963 season was the decision to use the full-court press the entire game, every game.

How sweet it is! Coach John Wooden and his Mighty Midgets celebrating their first national championship in 1964. It would become virtually an annual event for the next dozen years. Two celebrated players are kneeling in front—Walt Hazzard and Gail Goodrich.

Gail Goodrich letting one go from on high in 1964 play. Notice how blasé the fans are in the background. Ho-hum, another two points.

It is now known that UCLA coach John Wooden, the "Wizard of Westwood," was talked into using the press by his assistant, Jerry Norman. Wooden didn't think it would work, but he was willing to try.

And it didn't work. UCLA used the press to defeat Stanford for the conference title, forcing twenty turnovers. But the score was only 51–45. The turnovers didn't lead to much scoring. In the Arizona State game, the press was virtually useless. Immediately after that loss, Wooden and Norman began to study the errors of their ways. They had used a man-to-man or one-on-one press. It caused turnovers, but the effect was to slow the tempo of the game. It worked almost like a stall. Besides, the better guards were able to dribble around their defender and bring the ball up the floor without much inconvenience.

Out of the discussions between the two coaches came the revolution. At the opening of the 1964 season, UCLA unveiled the full-court *zone* press. Instead of playing opponents one on one, the Bruins played opponents in a portion of the floor or zone. At the crease of the zones, opponent guards found themselves facing two men, and it was impossible to dribble around both of them. They had to pass, and the other UCLA players picked off the passes like ripe apples on a tree—and scored. Another effect of the zone press was to open up the whole court, creating a wide-open style of play. But the biggest effect of the zone press was the panic it caused among opponents. Wooden and Norman sought to exploit human nature. As soon as a person makes a mistake, he instinctively rushes to correct it. The zone press forced errors. A guard is trapped far down the floor and there are only ten seconds to get the ball to midcourt. He has to pass over two pairs of frantically waving hands. He panics. He lobs a pass to a teammate. It is intercepted. Or he tries to dribble and loses the ball.

The full-court zone press created wholesale panic among opponents. Mistakes were rife, turnovers to UCLA a way of life. Ball control was impossible. Bringing the ball up the floor in an orderly fashion and running set plays for a score —forget it. Worse, momentum was always with the California team. It was racehorse, run, run, run basketball, with the Bruins reeling off ten and fifteen points in a row. Its effect was devastating, in part because it was a new wrinkle and in part because those UCLA midgets were just about the five quickest men ever to take the floor. Give them a chance to run on a wide-open floor and it was no contest.

Along with the full-court zone press, the Bruins began to play defense in earnest. Wooden committed himself to defense more than he had previously. His players learned that defense is more than standing between an opponent and his basket and waving the arms. Other than pass off, a player with a ball can do only one of three things; go to his right, go to his left, or shoot over the head of the defender. Good defense is forcing a player to do the thing he does least well. If he likes to dribble to his right—and four times out of five a right-handed player does that—the defender stands to the opponent's right, forcing him to go left. If there is a spot on the floor a player likes to shoot from, good defense doesn't let him get to that spot. There is a lot more to good defense, and the 1964 UCLA Bruins became superb college defensive players.

With good defense and the full-court zone press, the Bruins swept to the national championship in 1964 and in 1965. Those midgets beat some very good teams. Wooden became the Wizard. He turned the midgets into champions. He stressed defense, and he innovated the hated and feared press. He made key adjustments that turned defeat into victory. In the 1965 title game against the powerful Michigan team led by Cazzie Russell, the Wolverines were scoring al-

"The Wizard of Westwood," John Wooden, coaching his UCLA Bruins to victory. Chances are he is telling his charges to hold down the score.

most at will by getting the ball to Russell near the foul circle. Wooden called a time out and changed from a 2-2-1 zone to a 3-1-1 zone. This cut off the passing lane to Russell, and the Bruins went on to demolish Michigan.

Wooden was a master psychologist. Prior to the 1964 title game, rather than a long pep talk, Wooden quietly asked a single question: "Who can remember which team finished second in the NCAA two years ago?" The answer was Ohio State, but nobody could remember it. The point was not lost on the players. Who remembers losers?

UCLA doubtlessly fielded better teams, but a lot has to be said for that 1964 and 1965 team. It was perhaps best said by Aleksandar Nikolic, coach of the Yugoslav national team. On a tour of the United States in 1964, Nikolic saw UCLA play and remarked, as quoted by Dwight Chapin and Jeff Prugh in their biography of Wooden, *The Wizard of Westwood:* "Is small team. No big man, no big score. . . . But ziss—pardon, my English very bad—ziss is best I see. Because is *team.* All five." He held up five fingers. *"Team!* You understand? Is best!"

The 1966 Bruins were a disappointment. They were good enough, even ranked No. 1 in the nation for a while, but they lost the conference and never entered the NCAA tourney. Texas Western won the NCAA title in what was considered a rather off year for college basketball.

No one was concerned about that year's UCLA team, for waiting in the wings was a single, incredible basketball player, so good coaches and sportswriters were already conceding the next three national titles to UCLA. His name at that time was Lew Alcindor. Later he would embrace the Sunni sect of the Muslim religion and change his name to Kareem Abdul-Jabbar. Many consider him the finest all-around basketball player in history.

Jabbar was already a sensation in high school, Power

It's hard to believe, but that's Kareem Abdul-Jabbar in the act of blocking a shot. And the rim of the basket is ten feet off the floor! No wonder many consider him the greatest basketball player of all time. No. 42 coming up to help is Lucius Allen.

Memorial Academy, a Roman Catholic school in the heart of New York City. He was over seven feet tall, and a scoring machine. He was also quick and agile and a virtually solid wall on defense. In his four years at Power, he led his team to ninety-nine victories in a hundred games. More than two hundred colleges and universities sought him. Whatever team he played for would dominate college basketball. More than a hundred sportswriters were in attendance in May 1965 when he announced his choice: UCLA.

The 1966 freshman team at UCLA was a wonder. It included not only Jabbar, but also guard Lucius Allen, considered an outstanding professional prospect, which he turned out to be; Lynn Shackleford, a tremendous outside shooter known to his teammates as "the machine"; and Kenny Heitz, a fine defensive performer. The freshman team went undefeated. It even routed the national champion varsity, 75–60. The four freshman stars joined Mike Warren, a great playmaking guard, for the start of the 1967 season.

The predictions were correct. With Jabbar at low post, dominating the scoring and rebounding, UCLA swept to national titles in 1967, 1968, and 1969. These teams won eighty-eight of ninety games. The losses have turned out to be more memorable than the victories. One was to Elvin Hayes and the University of Houston in 1968. More than fifty-five thousand spectators jammed the Houston Astrodome to watch the upset, along with millions more on national television. Jabbar played with a scratched eyeball. UCLA avenged the loss in the NCAA semifinal game in Los Angeles in the spring. The other loss was to archrival Southern California later that season. The Trojans won, 46–44, using a stall to hold down the score.

With those two exceptions, nothing worked against Jabbar and the Bruins. A frequent tactic was to collapse two and three men around Jabbar under his own basket to keep him from scoring. This worked. Jabbar's point totals were held down from time to time. But that left the others open to score at will—Shackleford, Warren, Allen, Heitz, Jim Nielson, Curtis Rowe, Sidney Wicks, Edgar Lacey. Jabbar was the big man, a dominant force in basketball, the most celebrated player in the land, but the "other" four guys on the team were superb, too. UCLA was a powerhouse.

In many ways, however, the Jabbar-led teams, for all their greatness, were not classic UCLA teams. There were cliques. There was some friction and jealousy. Coach Wooden and Jabbar, for example, were never close. Jabbar was, and is, an introverted, complex individual. He had to cope with serious problems as a teen-ager. His height was enough to give anyone a complex. Then there was his celebrity status while he was still in high school. Most of all, Jabbar had to wrestle with his blackness. He had grown up in a comfortable middle-class home, not a ghetto. Yet he felt the pain of being black in a white world, and he struggled throughout his college days to express his individuality. He was a black, a person, not just a basketball freak. In a paid interview with *Sports Illustrated* while in college, Jabbar expressed his unhappiness at UCLA and confessed that he thought of transferring to other schools. He openly criticized Wooden in these words:

"He had this morality thing going; you had to be "morally" right to play. From that attitude came a serious inability on his part to get along with 'problem' players. If they didn't go to church every Sunday and study for three hours a night and arrive fifteen minutes early to practice and nod with every inspiring word the coach said, they were not morally fit to play—and they found themselves on the second team."

The frictions of the Jabbar era did not interfere with the

annual thrusts to the national title, largely because of the talent of the players, especially Jabbar. He was such a dominating player there was hardly any way that any team he played on could lose.

When Jabbar graduated in 1969 and went on to his superb professional career with the Milwaukee Bucks and the Los Angeles Lakers, few would have been surprised if UCLA went into a decline. But Jabbar's loss was hardly noticed as a marvelous Bruin team went on to two more NCAA championships. There almost seemed to be relief that Jabbar was gone. Wooden: "It will be fun coaching to win again, rather than coaching to try to keep from losing." Steve Patterson, who took over as varsity center, said of Jabbar: "No one is going to fill his shoes. It's going to take all of us, working together, to do that."

And they did just that. The team went back to its "old" style of racehorse, team-play basketball. There was Patterson, at six-nine, playing the high post. At forward were two superior players, inseparable on and off the court, Sidney Wicks and Curtis Rowe. The guards were John Vallely and Henry Bibby. This team didn't win big. It lost a few games, and it often had to scramble for victory. But it was a *team* of five outstanding players, playing together.

Most of that team graduated with the 1971 season, and the experts were certain the UCLA dynasty had ended. Not hardly, for Wooden assembled what he called his "greatest" team. There was Keith (Smooth as Silk) Wilkes, who specialized in "garbage" rebounds and hitting jump shots; Greg Lee, a slick passer; Larry (Moose) Farmer, a quick jumper and rebounder; and Larry Hollyfield and Tommy Curtis. Who played center? There was six-eleven Sven Nater. He made the United States Olympic team and much impressed foreign coaches. One asked Bob Boyd, the Southern Califor-

What really goes on under the basket is caught in this remarkable shot of 1971 play. No. 35, Sidney Wicks, and teammate Curtis Rowe fight off a quartet of New Mexico State players. The expressions on their faces tell the whole story.

The celebrated full-court zone press that revolutionized college basketball and terrorized opponents in the mid-1960s. No. 54 is Larry Farmer, later an assistant coach at UCLA. No. 45 is Henry Bibby, and No. 52, farther upcourt, is Keith Wilkes in this 1973 action shot.

Proud and talented, the 1970–71 Bruins and coaches pose for a formal team photo.

nia coach, "How do we stop him?" Boyd replied, "I can't tell you. We only see the *other* guy."

The other guy was Bill Walton. The most frequent and faintest praise of him is as "the best Caucasian center ever to play this game." Howie Dallman, the Stanford coach, said, "That kid destroys you." Carroll Williams of Santa Clara said, "He's the best college basketball player I've ever seen. He's better at both ends of the court than Lew Alcindor was—he dominates like no college player in the history of the game. And that includes Bill Russell, whom I played against." In 1977, Walton led the Portland Trail Blazers to the NBA championship. Shortly afterward Tommy Heinsohn, coach of the Boston Celtics, said of Walton: "He has brought a new dimension to the game. He just picks the defense apart. He's a playmaker par excellence—and at six-eleven. Nobody has ever played the position the way he does. And on defense he's the bottom of the funnel. It all derived from Bill Russell. But Walton has taken that concept and developed it superbly."

Strangely, Walton was not a particularly heralded high-school star, certainly not as Wilt Chamberlain and Lew Alcindor had been. Walton came from La Mesa, a suburb of San Diego, not an area noted for its basketball. Most basketball players seem to come from inner-city ghettos. New York turns them out by the dozen every year—or rather they turn themselves out from the asphalt playgrounds of Harlem, Bedford-Stuyvesant, and the South Bronx. Walton was red-haired and white-skinned. There hadn't been an outstanding white center since George Mikan a generation before. Last and most important, Walton had bad knees. He grew six inches between his freshman and sophomore years in high school and another three inches after that. The growth spurt left him with bad knees. He had an operation to repair torn cartilage when he was fifteen. He is

Bad knees and all, Bill Walton goes airborne to block this shot during 1973 play against the Wisconsin Badgers. No wonder it was an undefeated season for the Bruins.

bothered by gimpy knees to this day. At UCLA he had to use heat on them before the game, ice packs afterward. Many fear his professional career will be shortened because of it.

Walton led Helix High School to forty-nine straight triumphs, yet he was said to be slow to develop and didn't really come into his own till he arrived at UCLA. There he was merely devastating. The 1971 Bruins may have been the greatest ever. They won all thirty games and by an average of thirty-three points. In the two years the "Walton gang" stretched the victory skein to eighty-eight games before being upset on national television by a spirited Notre Dame team on January 19, 1974. The Fighting Irish lived up to that name. They overcame a huge deficit to win at the end. The Bruins avenged the loss two days later and went on to enter the NCAA playoffs. But the team, seeking its eighth straight championship, was obviously struggling. It lost in the semifinal to North Carolina State, led by seven-four Tom Burleson and brilliant forward David Thompson. NCS eventually won the title. The UCLA skein of national championships had ended. It was later learned that Walton had been playing with two cracked vertebrae in his back incurred in a hard fall twelve days prior to the Notre Dame game.

With the graduation of Walton, it would have seemed the UCLA dynasty was finally over. But one of the marks of a great team is the ability to rise from defeat and disappointment. The 1975 edition of the Bruins had Ralph Drollinger at center, Richard Washington, David Myers, Marquis Johnson, Andrew McCarter, and Pete Trgovich. It was a good team, but hardly overpowering, as the Walton and Jabbar teams. They had to scramble more, but scrambling had long been a hallmark of the more interesting UCLA teams.

The best college team in the country was Indiana. They were undefeated and ranked No. 1. In the NCAA semifinal they were upset by Kentucky, which entered the title contest against UCLA. The Bruins doubtlessly had an emotional edge. Before the game Coach Wooden announced this was to be his last game. He was retiring. His players wanted him to bow out a winner.

The game was low-scoring, indicating that defense was a priority. The Bruins put on a typical fourth-quarter surge and pulled away to a ten-point lead. Kentucky, possessors of their own great basketball tradition, fought back to within a single point. UCLA reasserted their dominance and won, 92–85, for the tenth national title in twelve years. After the game McCarter embraced his coach and spoke for the team and sports fans everywhere, "Coach, I hope you have a nice life."

The constant in the UCLA success was John Wooden. He was born in Centerton, Indiana, in 1910. He was an All-American guard at Purdue in the early 1930s, quite a dribbler and superbly conditioned. He was a successful high-school coach and a winning coach at Indiana State University. In 1948 he was recruited to coach at UCLA. Except for his first year as a high-school coach, Wooden had never played or coached a losing team. The 1948 Bruins had been last in the conference. The next year, Wooden's first, he made them a conference champion. In his first fifteen seasons at UCLA, it was a case of good, but not quite. His teams never had a losing season. They won eight division and conference championships, but no national titles. Then, when he was fifty-three, old as basketball coaches go, he won the first national title, and the string of NCAA championships began.

Much has been written about Coach Wooden. Much is made of his character and lifestyle. He has never drunk alcoholic beverages. He is a devoted family man, pious, morally straight. In the often swinging lifestyle of Southern California, he is a misplaced small-town midwestern boy.

One of the surprising elements of the UCLA string of national titles is the fact it coincided with the "youth rebellion." The mid-1960s were marked by great unrest on college campuses, draft protests, demonstrations against the war in Vietnam, and black power. UCLA was in the forefront of all these social and academic upheavals. Yet Wooden put together team after team that played together as a cohesive five-man unit.

The 1960s were also the years of drugs, love beads, lots of facial hair, and a swinging lifestyle. Wooden would tolerate little of it. He insisted on short hair, modest sideburns, and no beards. He wanted no drinking or smoking. His players were to dress well, act like gentlemen, get good grades, stay out of trouble, and be morally straight. Players who had trouble obeying these rules found themselves sitting on the bench or not making the team.

In return, Wooden gave his players a chance to win and win and win and a further chance for lucrative pro contracts. He was a father figure to many of his players as well as an authority figure, and he helped them with their scholastic and personal problems. Some players, such as Jabbar, felt distant from him. Others were extremely close. Walt Hazzard annually called Wooden on the eve of the NCAA tourney to wish him luck. Ron Pearson, a former player, calls Wooden "the finest man I ever met." Ex-UCLA chancellor Franklin Murphy says he has never known "a more honorable and decent human being."

Wooden was also fiercely competitive. Some of his battles with opposing coaches and referees are legendary. In one game he publicly castigated a sub for being slow to get up and enter the game. Angered, Wooden sat him back down on the bench. He felt the player hadn't shown the proper spirit. It was all a misunderstanding. The player was mentally gathering his thoughts to enter the game. Wooden had misread his intentions.

What makes a great team? Wooden: "I think all coaches would agree you must have talent. No one can win without it, but not everyone can with it. Once the talent is there, it must be disciplined into a team effort. The ways this is done depend upon the coaches's personality. After all, a coach is nothing more than a teacher or leader. There are many ways to do it. What worked for a Vince Lombardi or a Paul Brown or a Knute Rockne wouldn't work for me.

"I believe you have to make the players aware at the beginning that basketball is played by a *team,* not a collection of individuals. I always told my boys that I was interested in them only as basketball players who could help the team. When they left the floor, I was then interested in them as individuals. I also told them that when they walked on the basketball floor they were to think of nothing but basketball. When they walked off the floor, they were to forget it."

In recruiting players Wooden looked not so much for height or speed as for quickness. "There is a difference between quickness and speed, and I wanted players who were quick in comparison to others playing the same position. I would never sacrifice quickness for size." He also looked for a certain character in his players. "I wanted them spirited, but not temperamental. Does he have the unselfishness required for the team effort? Or if he appears to be selfish, can he change and learn the team concept? Many do change. We are able to get across to them that playing on a winning team will make them recognized for their individual talents."

Larry Farmer, former player and then assistant coach at

UCLA, says of Wooden, "He was by far the best coach in
the game. His rapport with the players, his ability to relate
to them and motivate them will never be duplicated."
Farmer said it was difficult to describe how Wooden took
twelve individuals and motivated them to become a team.
"I suspect he did many things. There was no one technique
for blending twelve totally different personalities into a
unit."

Wooden: "I didn't treat all the players alike. I sought to
give them the treatment they earned, deserved, and responded to. Nor did I like them all equally. There were
some I wouldn't have let date my daughter, for example.
Nor did the players like each other the same. There is no
way to have harmony all the time. Yet all that can and
should be forgotten on the floor. You can still have an excellent team effort from players who don't particularly care
for each other."

Farmer believes the weld for the teams was fashioned in
practice. "Games are won and lost in practice. We always
played against each other, older players vs. the younger,
and we tried to maintain the conditions that would occur in
the game. The team concept was learned there. The player
who didn't pass, didn't show the unselfishness to play as a
team, heard it from the coach." And as one player put it,
Wooden could make an expression like "goodness gracious"
resemble an Army-style chewing out. It is significant that
the criticism came only from the coaches. UCLA players
are forbidden to criticize each other's play. They may only
praise and encourage. This is the exact opposite of many
professional teams.

One of the secrets of the old New York Yankee baseball
teams was the knowledge of the players that being a Yankee meant winning. The carrot was to be a Yankee, the
stick was not to be a Yankee. Something similar happened

at UCLA. Farmer: "Our players learned that playing for UCLA meant playing for a winner. With the team concept they would all have the same recognition. All would be highly sought after by the pros. Kareem [Abdul-Jabbar] learned the team concept here. When his teammates got the ball and scored, the team won and all left the floor winners. Walton always was a fine team player and you can see that in Portland. Walton really doesn't care if he scores or not. He learned here that winning is what is important and it is the better team that wins. Sidney Wicks has had a difficult time in the pros simply because he is such a team player. His individual talents only shine in a team situation, and he has not had a team situation in the pros. Now that he has been traded to the Celtics, I believe he will fit splendidly into their team style of play. Bibby has had trouble adjusting to the pro style of play. Because the team concept is so ingrained into a UCLA player, many have difficulty adjusting to the more individualistic styles used by many pro teams."

Again, what is a team? Farmer: "It is the willingness of every guy to sacrifice his individuality, his ego to the goal of winning as a team." Wooden adds: "A good team playing as a unit will always beat five individuals, no matter how good they are. Portland's victory over Philadelphia in the [1977] NBA playoffs showed that."

Wooden-coached teams had a faculty for winning the important games that had to be won. He spoke of pressure and getting up for the big games. "I didn't want my players to be mad. I wanted them to have fire and determination, but to have it under control. You have to try harder when things are going poorly, but you have to control what you do. The good teams, having played a lot in competition, achieve a confidence. And I believe confidence comes from knowing you are in top physical condition, from certainty about your own skills, and from faith in your teammates."

Wooden's reference to confidence suggests that another factor is at work at UCLA. Perhaps the word for it is tradition. The Bruins play basketball at a lofty level. Where other teams hope for a winning season or a conference title, the Bruins seek a national championship. And not just once, when a super team comes along, but year after year. There is a standard of excellence at work in the Los Angeles school that has few equals. Every team needs a goal that cements the team together. The World Series, the Stanley Cup, the Super Bowl are goals in professional sports. College basketball provides such a goal with its NCAA tournament.

During its incredible skein of national titles, the Bruins twice had incomparably good big men, Jabbar and Walton. But in between them and in the year after Walton, the team still won. Shorter, perhaps even less talented men developed the drive and made the effort required to be the best in the land. A standard of excellence, a search for the impossible can be a strong weld for a team. It is often said that people set their goals too low and settle for less than they are capable of. Several teams of UCLA basketball players obviously never believed such nonsense.

OHIO STATE BUCKEYES

A significant number of major college football teams can be called dynastic. To name the most obvious: Penn State, Alabama, Grambling, Texas, Oklahoma, Southern California, Nebraska, Notre Dame, and Michigan. And the cries of outrage from a dozen other deserving unnamed schools are being heard loud and clear. Ohio State is clearly dynastic, fielding strong teams year after year, but why choose it? No thin argument of geography can be made this time. A half-dozen other midwestern teams are easily qualified. Clearly, as a native Ohioan and longtime Buckeye fan, I am open to a charge of rash, unmitigated chauvinism and ax-grinding. I plead innocent. I chose Ohio State because its coach is the most hated and loved, feared, controversial, and colorful coach in the land. But on the basis of results, he must be doing something right, or he was, until December 27, 1978, when his temper finally did him in. In the Gator Bowl and before a national television audience, he struck a Clemson University player who had just intercepted an Ohio State pass. Before the night was over, OSU had fired him. Yet he remains a legend.

How to Build a Machine

> He forces you to do your best all the time out of fear of
> what will happen if you don't.
>
> Bob Vogel

Woody Hayes. There are few sports fans in the United
States who will fail to identify him as the longtime football
coach at Ohio State. In 1977, he was beginning his twenty-
ninth year as head coach. He was the second winningest
coach, after Paul "Bear" Bryant at Alabama, among active
major college coaches. Only three college coaches in history
had won more games than Hayes: Glenn "Pop" Warner,
Amos Alonzo Stagg, and Bryant.

Not only is the name Woody Hayes well known, it also
propels an instant reaction. The man is either beloved and
admired, hated or endured. To his detractors, who are legion, Woody Hayes symbolizes in his ample physique everything that is wrong with high-pressure, must-win, big-time
college athletics today.

It is easy to caricature Woody Hayes. It has been done
many times. Here is a man in his mid-sixties, a full profes-

sor of physical education at one of the nation's leading universities, a teacher of young people, a man supposed to set an example for the youth of the nation, a man who puts great emphasis on personal discipline and fields such well-disciplined teams that they are often called a "machine," yet here is a man who regularly flies into uncontrollable rages. His assistant coaches and players measure his temper tantrums in "megatons," a term normally used to register the size of nuclear explosions. At their mildest, he swears like a lumberjack, if indeed lumberjacks cuss a great deal. He regularly rips off his wristwatch and stomps it under his feet. He takes off his eyeglasses and crushes them in his hand, ignoring the cuts that result. He takes off his baseball cap and rips it to shreds—or did until someone double-stitched it with heavy nylon so he couldn't tear it apart.

In his rages, he is said to have thrown typewriters and movie projectors. He has ripped phones out of the wall. He has shoved his hand through a blackboard because his team was behind at halftime. He regularly hits his own players in the belly or a ringing blow on the helmet. He has struck opposing players. A photographer has been felled. He decked a graduate assistant coach who just happened to be walking by him on the sidelines when something went wrong in a game. In a rage, he has punched himself so hard in the temples with both fists to blacken both his own eyes.

Nor is it just his rages that lend themselves to caricature. The football rivalry between Ohio State and the University of Michigan at Ann Arbor is well known, one of the most intense in the nation. Hayes refuses to say the word "Michigan," calling it "that school up North." Michigan State, another Big Ten rival, is the "other" school up North. A classic Hayes story has him and an assistant coach driving back from Michigan on a recruiting trip. The gas tank is nearly empty. Hayes will not let his assistant stop for gas because he will not contribute one cent in gas taxes to the state of Michigan. The vehicle sputtered and coasted across the state line into an Ohio gas station.

All this is fuel for the Hayes haters, suggesting an undisciplined, unstable character who is illogical and petty. Nor are these the only bases for lampooning Hayes. In the late 1960s and early 1970s, the era of protests against the war in Vietnam, he showed himself to be a superpatriot. His support for the war, his defense of his country right or wrong, his comparisons of football to military strategy, his wholehearted espousal of the eternal verities of Mom, flag, and country at a time when it was popular among a segment of the population to denigrate these things, gave his detractors ample material to ridicule him. In two words, Woody Hayes became famous and controversial as a coach and as a person.

To report these aspects of the Woody Hayes character is grossly unfair and misleading. As every one of his biographers points out, Hayes is a study in contrasts. This violent man treats his players as though they were his own sons, looks after their welfare as a whole person, not just as a football player. He regularly visits the sick in hospitals, and has a habit of befriending the discouraged and the down and out. The list of former players he has taken under his wing and helped guide back to a useful life is a long one. Jim Parker, former All-American at Ohio State and football Hall of Famer, recalls: "Woody recruited me. I was just a poor black kid who didn't know which way was up. I lived with Woody my first year at Ohio State. He was like a father to me, helping me scholastically and every other way. I remember one time I lost or had my four hundred dollars tuition money stolen. I went to him and told him just what had happened. He didn't doubt me, and he sure could have.

A celebrated sight—Coach Woody Hayes on the sidelines, shirt sleeves flapping, intent on another Ohio State victory. That 42–7 OSU lead, as recorded over his shoulder, perhaps accounts for Woody's more relaxed demeanor. At least the photographer got his picture. (*Photo by the Department of Photography and Cinema, The Ohio State University*)

He simply loaned me the four hundred dollars out of his own pocket. It's not everyone who'll do that."

Woody is said to work twenty-five hours a day at football, driving his assistant coaches and players to exhaustion with incessant study of films and drills on Ohio State plays. Somehow, though, he finds time to be an omnivorous reader. He is considered an authentic expert on history, particularly military history. He can talk by the hour about public affairs and social problems, then top it off by reciting poetry by the yard. A story is told of the time an OSU faculty member and a major detractor of Hayes buttonholed him to relieve himself of a long upbraiding of Hayes as a disgrace to the university. Hayes endured, then simply said, "That may be so, but I'll tell you. I can do your job but you can't do mine." Hayes's intellectual attainments are not to be taken lightly.

His football record is impeccable. Three of his teams have been national champions. Eleven teams won Big Ten titles, including four in a row. Eight of his teams played in the Rose Bowl, again including four in a row. His teams have won more than three quarters of their games. A list of the names of his assistant coaches who have excelled in their own right reads like a Who's Who of the gridiron— Ara Parseghian, formerly of Notre Dame; Bo Schembechler at Michigan; Carm Cozza at Yale; Lou Holtz at North Carolina State; Bill Mallory at Colorado; Earle Bruce at Iowa State; Paul Dietzel at South Carolina; John Pont at Northwestern; Bill Hess at Ohio University; Rudy Hubbard at Florida A&M. The pro ranks also include his former assistants. He has coached more college All-Americans and had more of his players drafted into professional football than any other coach.

Yet the record Hayes is most proud of is this: A higher percentage of his players graduate from college than any

Coach Woody Hayes (arm raised) has a few choice words for his Ohio State Buckeye players. All but the fellow in the foreground appear attentive. (*Photo by Chance Brockway*)

major football power in the land. Hayes is a nut on the academic achievements of his players. He cares more about their grade average than he does about their blocking and tackling. A classic Hayes story has him mountain climbing in the Italian Alps on a rare vacation. He phoned Columbus to inquire about a player known to have trouble with the books. When he found out the boy had flunked, Hayes chewed out every one of his assistants in succession, then topped off his rage by pulling the phone out of the wall and throwing it across the room. The next day he quit his vacation and flew home to remonstrate with the derelict player.

This list of Hayes contrasts is a long one. In the late 1960s and early 1970s, he worked tirelessly to quell the student riots that broke out at Ohio State. He went from dormitory to dormitory talking to students, trying to understand their complaints and to calm their anger. He is the lowest-paid major coach in the country—by far. He has consistently refused raises, while suggesting them for his assistants, as his contribution to the national treasury. Years ago he sold his car and walks two miles between his home and office as his personal contribution to protecting the environment and saving energy.

The list of Hayes stories is a long one. Every biography includes a great many of them. Face it: The man is a clump of contrasts. He is an eccentric, one of a kind. What is important about Woody Hayes is that these eccentricities are not poses. He believes them and practices them—daily. More importantly, Hayes's peculiarities, all those temper tantrums, petty foibles, flag-waving, insistence upon education and history reading are the precise ingredients by which he molds a collection of individuals into a team.

If the term "machine" has any accuracy in a sports contest, it is in Columbus, Ohio. The Buckeyes just grind out yardage. They play ball control. They run the same plays again and again. Opponents know what is coming, but that doesn't have much effect in stopping it. Woody Hayes's offense—and he is an offensive coach, leaving defense mostly to his assistants—has been lampooned as "three yards and a cloud of dust." The most famous single play in the land is "Fullback 26, right or left." It is the play Hayes most often sends into the huddle, a sheer power play with the fullback—and Ohio State has had so many great full-backs it is often called a "fullback college"—bruiting into the line, right or left of the center. The only question is which tackle the fullback is going to hit. It is basic football. It is highly physical football, muscle against muscle. In the pros, Vince Lombardi and the great Green Bay Packer teams were most famous for this brand of football.

Consider it no joke. There is method to this style of play. For starters, Hayes likes to run these power plays right at the opponent's strength. If the defense has a great tackle and linebacker on the left side, rest assured that is where the play is going to go. Early in the game, Hayes will run his power plays right at the strength and most of the time overpower it. It is a psychological bombshell for the defense to know its best is not good enough.

Hayes has what to him are valid reasons for Fullback 26. It is not an easy way to win. It is the hard way, and he considers that good for the character of his players. Also, the fullback cannot gain four or five yards on his own. The whole offensive team must block for him. He considers it a play that builds team spirit.

More, the off-tackle play works. Hayes sent graduate as-sistant coach Bill Davies off to find out what really wins a football game. After examining forty games in the Big Ten, Davies discovered that the team that gains more yardage rushing wins the game 90 per cent of the time. The team with the higher average gain per rush wins 85 per cent of the time, as does the team with the higher average gain per play. The team with more total yardage wins 82.5 per cent of its games, the team with more rushing attempts wins 80 per cent of the time, and the team with more rushing first downs wins more than three quarters of the time.

In contrast, the team with the higher passing completion percentage and higher average gain per completion wins little more than half the time. Net yardage passing wins only 40 per cent of the games, and the team throwing more passes wins 15 per cent of the time. Hayes knew it all along. As he puts it, only three things can happen to a pass, and two of them are awful: an incompletion and an interception. Hayes practices a pass attack. It has its uses, to keep a defense from stacking up on rushing plays. Passes may be needed late in a game when Ohio State is behind. If he has a good passing quarterback, such as Rex Kern, he has been known to pass as many as twenty-five or thirty times a game. But even then it is only halfhearted. A pro-type pocket passer wouldn't play at Ohio State. Hayes runs his pass plays off the option, disguising the pass as a run and most often continuing it as a run.

The machinelike qualities of an Ohio State football team stem from a single thing: practice. The Ohio State playbook is a skimpy affair. The players are never burdened, as on many pro teams, with memorizing hundreds of plays and formations. The Buckeyes have very few plays, perhaps no more than a half dozen basic ones. Jim Parker: "He would have us practice the same plays, off tackle and end run, by the hour. We might run the same play a thousand times vs. every conceivable defense that might be developed against it. There was nothing to do but run those plays. It became second nature. On lots of teams, guys are worrying about whether the other guy is going to do his job. We never had any such worries. We just knew everybody was going to do his job."

Bob Vogel, All-American at Ohio State: "Hayes would run the same play again and again until the whole team could execute it perfectly. And in a game we'd run the same play, again and again until we wore out our opponents. We had so few basic plays and we ran them so many times, there was little chance for error. We didn't have to think. It was automatic. In a word, we were consistent. As Hayes taught us, if we ran a play ten times and it succeeded six times, that was bad. We ran plays till it was executed perfectly ten times out of ten."

Rex Kern, star Ohio State running-passing quarterback and former pro with the Baltimore Colts: "In practice, Hayes would have us run the same off-tackle, Fullback 26 play as many as twenty-five times in a row. It was never quite right for him. I know what he was doing. Football is a game of reaction. We ran the same play so often we just reacted. None of us had to think about what we were doing. More importantly, running the same play made us a team. You should have heard the griping and the groaning. The same play, again and again, time after time. We would get so mad at him we were determined to show him. We'd run the play so well he'd have to let us practice another play. Our anger at him, our weariness at the same play, our determination to get it right to please him brought us together as a team. And don't think Woody Hayes didn't know that was happening."

Hayes's practices are celebrated. He is considered a master organizer. Parker: "If practice was supposed to start at one forty-five, that's when it started—sharp—and not a second was wasted." Hayes has his players suit up, both in practice and in pregame warmups. He wants them used to wearing those pads. He drills daily on such fundamentals as block-

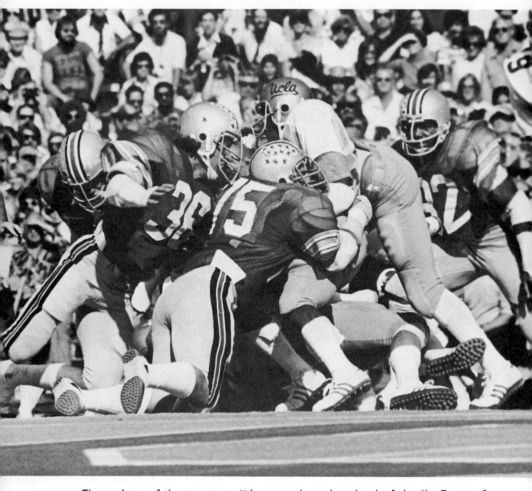

Three views of the awesome "three yards and a cloud of dust" offense of
the Ohio State Buckeyes.
(*Photo by Malcolm W. Emmons*)

(Photo by Chance Brockway)

ing and tackling, for to him they are what the game is all about. Vogel: "When I came with the Colts, I was more technically proficient in the fundamentals of the game than 98 per cent of the players from other colleges." Hayes has them hit hard in practice—"hit and fit" in football parlance —so they are used to game conditions. This is part of conditioning. OSU players are at their best late in a game when opponents are tired.

Much is done to simulate game conditions. Two doctors are in attendance at practice to treat injuries. There is a dentist, too, and a dentist chair in the locker room for emergency treatment. Hayes spends several thousand dollars a year paying accredited game officials to participate in practice. In a scrimmage, the officials call the penalties as they would in the game. Ohio State loses very little yardage in penalties.

Practice scrimmages are filmed so players are not only chewed out by an enraged Hayes, but they also can see their mistakes on film—again as in a real game. Younger players, not yet ready to make the varsity, play on special teams trained in opponents' plays, either offense or defense. They are outfitted with jerseys of the opponents' team and even the same numbers. Hayes wants his players *thoroughly* familiar with what they will face come Saturday.

A special part of every practice is devoted to the kicking game—often neglected by other coaches. Hayes feels kicking is important to football, and he intensely practices punting, place kicking, kickoffs, and punt and kickoff returns. It is a rare day in September, on the category of never, that Ohio State is scored upon with a punt or kickoff return or has a punt blocked.

Like John Wooden at UCLA, Hayes believes games are won in practice. He wants his teams to know the fundamentals, to be in superior condition, and to have executed the basic plays so often they have total confidence in their ability to run those plays and in their teammates. There is a bit more. Hayes knows that all players do not learn at the same rate of speed. Some will learn quickly and become bored, while others simply take longer. Hayes wants *all* to know the plays equally well, and he wants those who know them well to learn to execute without letting down. The Ohio State machine. It often is.

In the back of this tireless effort on the field is the tireless effort of the coaching staff. Hayes drives himself relentlessly, and his assistants just as hard. They spend hours looking at films of opponents' games each week, studying their offensive and defensive plays, keeping statistics on which play they run in certain situations, searching for "keys" to which play is being run (arrangement of linebackers, how offensive linemen set their feet, etc.), probing for a pattern, a weakness that can be exploited.

Out of this comes a "game plan," a series of plays, both offensive and defensive, that can be practiced all week and are most likely to work. To Hayes, these are the secrets of the game. To suggest that the physical endurance of his assistants will give out before these secrets have been discovered is to witness Hayes in a rage. The stories are legion. Yet Hayes entrusts responsibility to his assistants. They know the OSU players and the game situation. Mostly he relies on their judgment.

An Ohio State game is an army marching into battle or maybe a machine primed for its fullest functions. A battery of coaches is in the press box, studying opponent formations and taking Polaroid photographs of the enemy the instant each play is run. The offensive or defensive play most likely to succeed is sent down to Hayes from above, because these coaches have the best view. He overrules a few, but generally he goes along. The play is sent in to the quarterback through a substitute. Hayes feels the quarterback has enough to do seeing that the formations are correct without thinking of the plays, too.

When Ohio reaches the opponents' ten-yard line, Hayes takes over the offense. He seems to will his players across the goal line. He calls all the plays, only occasionally listening to his frustrated coaches stationed above. On play after play, he orders POWER—Fullback 26 or the famous OSU end sweep. It becomes a case of Woody Hayes against the enemy, with the players becoming mere executors of his personal will to win. You may stop Ohio State at midfield, but inside the ten it is something else, the execution of an enemy by a dominant personality.

None of these—the practices under game conditions, the repetition of a single play, the search for game plans, the photography, and the coaches in the press box—are the secrets to Ohio State success. All of these can be and are duplicated elsewhere. What is unique about Ohio State football lies in the personality of Woodrow Wilson Hayes.

He truly believes in Mom, God, and country. He really does read history and humanities. He really does love people, and he wholeheartedly believes that playing football and winning is the greatest possible development of the human character. He came to Ohio State in 1948. He had been a small-time Ohio high-school coach who had done well at Miami of Ohio. Another former Miami coach was considered a shoo-in for the job at OSU, Paul Brown, former coach at Massillon High School, Miami, OSU, and then the Cleveland Browns, where he built a dynastic team. In recent years, Brown has been with the Cincinnati Bengals. Many rank Brown among the greatest coaches in the history of football. He was supposed to return to Ohio State in 1948. His personal following was immense. There were demonstrations urging his return. The university chose Hayes. Who?

Hayes was a knowledgeable football coach, but wasn't everyone? About the only thing going for him was that he was considered a good recruiter for Miami of Ohio. Hayes is still a good recruiter. At Ohio State it is his main business.

Vogel: "One of the secrets of Ohio State football is the location of the university in one of the great available pools of talent." True. High school football in Ohio is a disease. There are fifty teams in the large and small towns of Ohio that play first-class scholastic football. The state of Ohio annually stocks the football teams of the nation. There is probably no way in which Ohio State can field a bad team, but they wouldn't be as good as they are if it weren't for Woody Hayes.

It will sound familiar to readers of this book: Yankee character, selecting the right players to achieve the teamwork of the Celtics, UCLA Bruins, and Colts. At Ohio State selecting the right player is known as looking for the "quality kid." Hayes looks for the boy, black or white, who comes from a "good home." He wants them big and fast and experienced in the off-tackle play, but more than that, he wants them to have enjoyed a "good home life." This means the parents are in the home. The family is closely knit. The members share common interests. Kern: "Hayes looks for the family that eats together, goes to church together, attends athletic contests together. He wants the boy who has the strong support of his mother and father, sisters and brothers."

When he finds such a boy, and the country is full of them, Hayes is tireless in visiting these families. Usually he doesn't talk football very much. He is eloquent about history, poetry, and the eternal verities. He tells them what a great education is available at Columbus. He wants them to know education is first; football, second. The parents lap it up. The players lap it up.

Hayes is a recruiting genius. He considers it suitable material for a hundred-megaton rage to have a talented Ohio boy to go to a school out of state. If he chooses that school "up North," try not to be in the room with the OSU coach. The prospective tackle or fullback is given a rush worthy of a sorority candidate. He is invited to Ohio State games along with his dad, given good seats, invited to the locker room, and presented with ample opportunity to bask under the spell of Woody Hayes. Jim Parker: "The team spirit at Ohio State begins the moment you walk into that stadium in Columbus. You see that big horseshoe filled with eighty-seven thousand fans, see the marching band, the pageantry, and you want to play at Ohio State—do you ever!"

Rex Kern believes the talk about good family background and the importance of graduating from college are important means by which Hayes creates teamwork. "Everyone comes from a similar background. All share his ideals. All work toward common goals. It makes his teams pull together as a unit."

Nor is the business about the school "up North" and his penny pinching about gasoline in Michigan just the foibles of an eccentric. Kern: "From the start of fall practice, Hayes has his teams working toward the goal of winning the Michigan game. It creates another bond that unifies the team."

Hayes's former players say he treats everyone alike. He wants all to succeed in football and in college. For years he has handed out tiny decals in the shape of a buckeye, the nut-shaped state emblem. These are awarded after each game to men who made great plays. The decals adorn the helmets and are much coveted. Hayes uses these decals as a way to give recognition to linemen and players on specialty teams who seldom make the headlines or the statistical tables. Another form of recognition is to post the photographs of the outstanding players in the locker room each week. These are seldom seen by the general public, but they mean a lot to the players.

Along with these carrots comes a stick. Hayes is seldom satisfied. He drives every player to perform at the utmost of his ability. A fullback or halfback may have gained two hundred yards the previous Saturday, but Hayes will find some aspect of his game that needs improvement. He didn't block as well as he could have. He missed an assignment on a play or two. And these criticisms are made at open meetings. If the good players are criticized, little imagination is needed to foresee what happens to the player who did poorly or, heaven help him, goofed off or failed to try his best.

Woody Hayes's celebrated temper is a major way in which he instills teamwork. He treats everyone alike—a punch in the belly, a swat on the helmet, a first-class dressing down in front of his teammates, or a display of spectacle-breaking and wristwatch-stomping. Vogel: "Woody Hayes is a very intimidating guy. He intimidates you physically, mentally, and every other way. He forces you to do your best all the time out of fear of what will happen if you don't. I must say, however, that I got little of this treatment from him. I have always been my own worst critic. I was never satisfied with my play and I was always on myself to do better. Coach Hayes knew this and pretty much left me alone." Kern: "I was never once hit by Hayes, and I was atypical in that. At one time or another he hit everybody. He'd swat them. I even saw him rip the jersey off players in his anger.

But he knew he didn't need to do that sort of thing with me. I guess you might say he sort of fathered me."

The secret of Hayes's rage is that it passes quickly. Psychologists viewing him in action point out that he is such an obviously physical person that he needs an outlet for his anger, hence the hitting and stomping and throwing of objects. The anger dissipates as quickly as it is physically expressed. No degree in psychology is needed to realize that Hayes is able to get away with some outrageous behavior because everyone on his team and everyone associated with Ohio State football know that Hayes truly loves his boys and wants only the best for them as well as from them. The rage without the family verities and the thrust for scholastic achievement would have meant a short, if eventful, coaching career for Hayes.

There are doubtlessly many factors involved in the dynastic success of Ohio State football teams. All Ohioans follow the team. Columbus goes football mad in the fall. More than eighty-seven thousand people pack the stadium at each home game to root the team to victory and to ooh and aah over the superb Ohio State marching band. Those huge crowds, plus their share of television rights, away-game receipts, and bowl appearances make football highly profitable for the university. There is no shortage of money for athletic scholarships, recruiting expenses, and the best in equipment. The very success of Ohio State football means that the best prospects want to play for the Buckeyes. Starring at OSU often brings a lucrative pro contract.

All of these are factors in the OSU dynasty, but the most important factor is Woody Hayes. He is a good coach, knowledgeable about the game and coaching techniques. His players are well conditioned and primed on the fundamentals. But lots of coaches do this. What makes Woody Hayes so successful is his uniqueness. He is one of a kind in those temper tantrums, his emphasis on family life, on graduating from college, on doing your best at all times, and on practice, practice, practice till the very best is automatic. The Ohio State football machine is formed from the nuts and bolts of Hayes's personality, his intimidation, and his demand for excellence in all things.

MONTREAL CANADIENS

In fifty seasons, from 1927 through 1977, Montreal finished either first or second in league competition thirty-four times. At the end of regulation play, the top teams square off for the Stanley Cup. In those fifty years, the Canadiens have won the Stanley Cup eighteen times. They lost in the finals six other times and in the semifinal round another thirteen times. In those fifty years, the Canadiens have been out of the playoffs precisely four times. Nor is this a record achieved in earlier years. Montreal won the Stanley Cup in 1976, 1977, and 1978.

The Importance of Fans

> If you have a bad game . . . you simply don't go out of
> the house afterwards.
>
> Maurice "Rocket" Richard

What is the roughest sport in terms of physical demands on
the players and pure mayhem? There are lots of claimants.
Boxing, certainly. Football produces many injuries despite
all the pads and gear worn. Basketball has a lot of rough
stuff, and none of the players are wearing protective equipment. The same can be said for soccer. Baseball, too. Many
purists claim the roughest sport is a somewhat obscure one,
box lacrosse.

It is hard, however, to argue against ice hockey. The
players wear protective gear, all right. It would be murder
if they didn't. The ice the game is played on is far harder
than a football field or a basketball floor. Two-hundred-
pound men crash into each other—body checking, it is
called—at speeds of twenty, thirty, even forty miles an
hour. Through the air flies a hard rubber puck at speeds up
to one hundred miles an hour. Worse, the men are armed.

On their feet are the approximate equivalent of knives. In their hands is a wooden stick. It has a lot more menacing uses than propelling the puck.

Under the most ideal circumstances, with the combatants acting like true sportsmen, hockey is a dangerous sport. The problem is these ideal circumstances are an increasing rarity. The game itself encourages mayhem. Body checking leads to flared tempers, open fist fights, promises of vengeance. The psychology of the game suggests that rough stuff, even if it results in time in a penalty box, is better than allowing a goal to be scored. Flattening an opponent, even injuring him, is considered a valuable strategy, for it intimidates him and his teammates, making them cautious. Hockey is no game for the faint of heart. It demands the attitude of the bully and the street brawler as much as the ability to skate.

Professional ice hockey is in trouble. In the 1960s, the number of teams expanded greatly with the formation of the World Hockey Association and the addition of teams to the National Hockey League. Most of these teams are losing money. Worse, the stock of players of professional quality is spread extremely thin. Almost all the players come from Canada, where hockey is the national sport. Where American boys throw a baseball or football, a Canadian boy laces on his skates and heads for the pond or rink. Canada is a virtual mine of hockey players, but Canada has a population of only about twenty-three million, roughly the size of the population of California or New York State. There just aren't enough quality Canadian players to stock all those professional teams. Thus the teams have been filled out with players who offer more muscle and mayhem than skill.

Believing that fans want to see fights and bloodshed more than ice hockey, team owners and managers, coaches and players have been willing to provide the mayhem in abundance. The classic hockey play of a superb skater racing down the ice and feinting a defender out of position to attack the goal with the puck has been replaced with a thinly disguised tackle and a left hook to the jaw. The situation is so serious that there is even talk of legislating rule changes and making hockey players criminally responsible for their physical assaults in the game. Many fans are deeply worried about the deterioration of the sport.

Deteriorated or no, the sport is unchanged in one respect. It is still dominated by a single team, Les Canadiens of Montreal. No team, not even the Yankees in baseball, has dominated a sport so long and so thoroughly as the Canadiens. Like so many of its predecessors, the current club is being called the "greatest ever."

That is an accolade calculated to start an instant argument in downtown Montreal or anywhere else in the province of Quebec. Old-timers will argue that real hockey was played by men such as Newsy Lalonde and Georges Vezina before the 1920s or by Howie Morenz, George Hainsworth, Johnny Gagnon, and Aurel Joliat in the 1930s. A superlative team was fashioned in the 1940s under coach Dick Irvin. Its line of Toe Blake at left wing, Elmer Lach at center, and Maurice Richard at right wing was one of the most devastating ever formed. Bill Durnan was in the crease. Kenny Reardon and Emile Bouchard regularly made the NHL All-Star team.

As great as this team was, few will argue that it was surpassed by the roster that reeled off five consecutive Stanley Cup victories from 1956 through 1960. Toe Blake, who had been named coach, fashioned perhaps the greatest single trio ever to form a forward line: Bernie "Boom Boom" Geoffrion, Jean Beliveau at center, and "Rocket" Richard. The rest of the roster included such luminaries as the Rocket's younger brother Henri "The Pocket" Richard,

When you've been an All-Star player and one of the winningest coaches in history, you get to celebrate like this. Toe Blake of the Montreal Canadiens letting everyone know how happy he is. (*Photo by Willie Dagenais*)

Jacques Plante in goal, Doug Harvey, Tom Johnson, Bert Olmstead, Ken Mosdel, Dickie Moore, Phil Goyette, Don Marshall, Ralph Marshall, Claude Provost, Bill Hicke, and Ralph Backstrom. Even the subs would have been first string on other teams.

The Canadiens of this era were merely the best of some very good teams in what was perhaps the golden age of hockey. Detroit iced powerful teams led by Gordie Howe. The Toronto Maple Leafs had "Wild Bill" Ezinicki and other great stars. The Chicago Black Hawks had the incomparable Bobby Hull. The Canadiens were dominating at a time when superlative hockey was played.

Of all these players the most celebrated was Maurice Richard (pronounced ree-SHARD). Perhaps no player in history so dominated a major sport as the Rocket did hockey for eighteen seasons, from 1942 to 1960. There have been better all-around players than he—including, many feel, his younger brother Henri—but Maurice Richard is considered the greatest scorer the game has ever known, with 626 goals lifetime. In 1944–45, he scored fifty goals in a fifty-game season. He once scored eight points in a single game, five goals and three assists. He performed the "hat trick" of scoring three goals in a game twenty-six times in regular-season play and seven more times in playoffs. He twice scored four goals in a game and once five in a game. Three times he scored three goals in a single period. He also had three assists in a single period, five assists in a game.

Perhaps the greatest measure of Richard was as a clutch performer. One hundred and one times he scored the winning goal for Montreal, including eighteen winning goals in playoffs, six of those in overtime. It was his performance under pressure that made him a living legend. Canadiens fans still recall his performance in the 1944 playoffs. Mont-

A living legend, Maurice "The Rocket" Richard brings the puck down the ice.

real had dominated the play that season, losing only five games and tying seven in a fifty-game schedule. They were twenty-five points ahead of second-place Detroit and thirty-three ahead of Toronto. Yet the Maple Leafs stunned Montreal with a 3–1 victory in the first playoff game. The second game started no better, with a scoreless first period. Then in the second minute of the second period, Richard, taking a pass from defenseman Mike McMahon, scored the first goal for the Canadiens. Fifteen seconds later the crowd was brought to its feet when Richard, set up by his companions on the "Punch Line," Elmer Lach and Toe Blake, scored again. The Maple Leafs scored, but Richard got it back with his third goal before the period ended. Before the first minute of the third period had passed, Richard had his fourth goal. His fifth came shortly before the end of the game. Final score: Richard 5, Maple Leafs 1. Montreal went on to rout Toronto and win the Stanley Cup.

Richard earned his nickname for the speed with which he skated, his daring and fearlessness in approaching the net, and his single-minded determination to score. He had the "killer instinct" for scoring. The impossible shot was his forte, particularly under pressure. Goalie Frank Brimsek said of him: "He can shoot from any angle. You play him for a shot to the upper corner and the Rocket wheels around and fires a backhander into the near, lower part of the net." Boston's Murray Henderson: "When Richard breaks on one defenseman, there's no telling what he'll do. If he gets his body between you and the puck, you just can't get at it. He cradles the puck on the blade of his stick, steers it with one hand, and wards off his check with the other. Strong? That guy is like an ox, but he sure doesn't look it."

A common scene was for a defenseman, as he should, to force the Rocket too far to the side to get a shot at the net.

Richard's answer was to veer sharply to his left as he drew abreast of the net. That still left an impossible shot, but he could make it because he shot left-handed.

The principal tactic against Richard was brute force. Perhaps no player in hockey had so many fierce body checks, had so many high sticks aimed at him, or endured so many punches and wrestling holds as Richard. Unable to stop him within the rules, opponents conspired to stop him any way they could. It may not have been true, as Richard fans insisted, that opponents tried to get him out of the game by physically injuring him, but certainly every effort was made to get him into the penalty box as much as possible. This worked. Richard spent 1,473 minutes in the penalty box during his career. That's the equivalent of more than 24 hours in punishment. Richard was moody, temperamental, competitive, and possessed of a temper. He was also very good with his fists. It was suggested, after he decked the same player twice in one game, that he ought to take up boxing as a career. The aim of the rough play by opponents was to goad Richard into fighting back. That was not difficult. He felt the need to defend himself and to revenge the assaults on himself. This brought on some classic brawls and lots of penalties.

The complaint of the Montreal fans was that referees were quick to see the punches thrown by Richard, but rather blind to the attacks on Richard that aggravated his anger. An example of this occurred near the end of the 1954–55 season. The Canadiens were leading the league and favored for the Stanley Cup when they tangled with the Bruins at Boston. The Bruins were not considered one of the better teams that year, but they were one of the roughest. For the first two periods, the Bruins roughed up the Canadiens. In the locker room, Coach Dick Irvin urged his team to come out fighting. Many of them, notably the

Rocket, did just that. Soon Hal Laycoe, a former Montreal player, crashed into Richard and opened a bloody cut in his scalp. The Rocket got up fighting, but Laycoe had the sense to retreat.

His temper flaring, Richard continued in pursuit, but was intercepted both by his teammates and linesman Cliff Thompson, a former Boston defenseman who lived in the Boston area. Instead of pushing Richard away, Thompson used a series of wrestling holds on him, which led to Richard and the official going to it on the ice.

Richard went to the penalty box and the incident seemed forgotten until the Boston newspapers began to scream for Richard's head the next day. This led to a hearing before league commissioner Clarence Campbell. There was a history of league fines and suspensions against Richard, which Montreal fans considered unfair. After the latest incident, Campbell shocked hockey by suspending Richard for the rest of the season, including the playoffs.

Without Richard, the Canadiens had no chance to beat out the Detroit Red Wings for first place or defeat them in the playoffs. Montreal fans were enraged. Several threats were made against Campbell's life. Yet the commissioner had the courage to show up at the Forum in Montreal to watch a Richardless team play the Red Wings. As Campbell took his seat, he was physically attacked. A melee developed as police moved in to try to protect the commissioner. A rain of programs, tomatoes, and other debris fell on the ice. In the middle of this someone exploded a canister of tear gas. The arena was evacuated and the game forfeited to Detroit.

Campbell escaped through a rear door, but barely, as the enraged hockey fans went on a rampage of burning, looting, and vandalism in downtown Montreal. Damage from the St. Patrick's Day riot was estimated at a hundred thou-

Jean Beliveau shows the form that made him one of the most feared players ever to take the ice. He is now an executive with the Canadiens.

sand dollars. Along with his more notable achievements, Richard is one of the few men in sports ever to cause a full-blown riot. In his defense, he went on radio and television to plead with Montrealers to accept Campbell's decision and to look forward to next season.

The St. Patrick's Day riot may not be one of the shining moments in the history of Montreal sports, but it does contribute to an understanding of why the Canadiens have dominated hockey for so long. Jean Beliveau, longtime center and captain of the team and now its director of public relations: "It is the dream of every youngster in the province of Quebec to wear this uniform."

There is no doubt that this is true, for hockey is an obsession in Canada. Canadians believe the sport was invented there. It is their own, an expression of national pride, much as baseball, football, and basketball are in the United States. Other countries, no matter how adept at the sport, are Johnny-come-latelies in the game, mere imitators. Canada abounds with ponds and indoor rinks. A child learns to skate almost as soon as he learns to walk. Schoolboys play on organized teams. Junior hockey for teen-agers flourishes, and many Canadians argue that some of the most exciting hockey is played by juniors. There are organized senior and semipro leagues, with professional hockey seeking out the best players.

All of this is highly organized, so much so that it is difficult for the people of the United States to fully appreciate the attention lavished on minor-league hockey. After all, our minor-league baseball and football suffer because of the impact of major-league play. In contrast, Jean Beliveau was a celebrity in the city of Quebec long before he signed with the Canadiens. It was difficult for him to give up his status in Quebec for the vagaries of the NHL.

Because so much hockey is played by so many people in

Canada, the fans are extremely knowledgeable. It is not just a case of rooting the home team to victory, but also expertly judging the players' performances. The fans *know* hockey and can judge whether a player did well or poorly. Even in defeat, fans can still cheer their team for having played well or admire an opponent's skill. Perhaps the best parallel to this fan expertise is in Europe and South America, where soccer is played so widely that the spectators are all experts.

There is an added dimension to this role of the fans in Montreal. The province of Quebec is the French-speaking part of Canada. The French explorers and settlers were among the earliest in North America. The province may have been conquered by the British, but the people of Quebec have held to their Frenchness ever since. French is the dominant language; for many people it is the only language. The people of Paris can understand French Canadian, but consider it archaic, unchanged by modern usage. French Canadian, to a Parisian, sounds a little like Elizabethan English would to British or Americans.

More than language separates the French of Quebec from the rest of Canada. They seethe under what they believe to be economic, social, and political discrimination by the English-speaking Canadians, particularly from Ontario. There is a strong strain of ethnic pride among the people of Quebec and a pronounced desire for separatism. Many observers are convinced that Quebec will eventually declare its national independence from Canada.

Hockey has a role in this. The Montreal Canadiens are not just any old sports team. They are the pride and joy of the people of Quebec. They are an expression of ethnic pride and nationalistic spirit. Whether they wish it or not, members of the team play not just to win or for money or

A fine action shot around the Canadiens' net. No. 21 is Doug Jarvis. But of even greater fascination is the reaction of the Montreal fans, perhaps the most dedicated and critical in all of sports. (*Photo by Michel Ponomareff*)

the motives of other sports teams, but to express the nationalistic feelings of Quebec.

These factors make the Montreal Canadiens unique in
sports. Rocket Richard: "If you have a bad game, particularly if you lose, you simply don't go out of the house after-
wards. You not only are criticized for your bad play in the
newspapers and on radio and television, you are also
accosted on the street. The people tell you how bad you
were and ask what's the matter with you. This is the most
pressure I know. It makes you play harder just to avoid the
public criticism after the game." Beliveau: "The fans exert
a lot of pressure on the players. You must give a good performance. The fans know what you can do. If you do not
perform up to expectations, it is not long before they let
you know it." Toe Blake: "The whole province takes a big
interest in our hockey team. They don't hesitate to speak
their minds. I think it makes a very healthy pressure on the
players."

It is difficult to think of a parallel in the United States.
Many American fans are knowledgeable about our major
sports. Yet much of the excellence of a player's performance is lost. A double play in baseball is extremely difficult
to execute, yet it is taken for granted by fans. Much of the
exotic expertise of football is lost on the fans. The result is
appreciated, but the subtle formations, the pass patterns,
precise timing, pass rushes, blocks, and so forth are often
so much mumbo jumbo to season ticket holders. Basketball
fans can appreciate the fast break, the rebound, and the
jump shot. But the intricacies of defense, the switchoffs, the
shoving for position under the basket are things seldom appreciated. Not so in Montreal. The fans know the game of
hockey. Nor are performances by American athletes so publicly criticized as in Canada. Sports are games, forms of en-
tertainment in the United States, not expressions of nation-

alism. We will boo bad performances, such as a batting slump, but fail to recognize the many other contributions made by a player in the field. We often boo a player for emotional reasons, including his high salary.

Clearly, fans do contribute to the success of a team— and, equally clearly, no more than in Montreal. Imagine Maurice Richard afraid to leave the house because he played poorly in his last game.

There is another factor involved. Richard: "I believe an important, frequently overlooked factor in the success of the Canadiens is the fact the players live at home. They live with their families, their wives and children. They live orderly and correctly among their friends and neighbors." Most of the professional hockey players in the United States are Canadian. Even when players on the U.S. teams are playing "at home" games, the players are away from home, families, familiar surroundings. For them, an "at home" game is in Toronto or Montreal. Richard: "There are many good players on the teams in the United States, but being away from home, living in hotel rooms and apartments while their families are in Canada has a bad effect. By the middle of the season they seem not as good as at the beginning. They are not in as good condition, nor is their mental attitude as good. I think this gives a big advantage to Montreal and Toronto."

Former Canadiens give another reason for the team's success: the organization behind the team. Richard: "We have good owners, good general managers." Toe Blake: "Our success stems from the whole organization, players, coaches, managers, directors. Everyone came up through the organization. The kids on the rinks have always been looked after. For years and years we kept a monopoly on the best players and that came from the organization of the club itself. We have always been a big happy family." Beliveau:

"Everybody is involved, not just the players. We've had very good managers. We've been very successful in the draft. We work very well with junior players. Everyone accepts his responsibility to the team's success and gives full effort. The success of the Canadiens is a common effort by everyone. When a youngster joins the organization, it is up to him to maintain the brand of hockey we play. It is his responsibility to maintain the Canadiens as the best team." Toe Blake again: "I cannot say too much about our being a big happy family. Everyone came up through the system and knows the system. Everyone knows what everyone gets paid. I don't know any team in any sport that is as close together as we are."

The Canadiens have had a remarkable continuity of organization. The ownership has changed, but that has had little effect. There have been few general managers over the years of the dynasty: Frank Selke in the fifties, Sam Pollack ever since. Dick Irvin was coach for many years, then Toe Blake beginning in 1955, Claude Ruel in 1968, and Scotty Bowman beginning in 1971. Former players often find a place in the organization, as befits a family institution.

Blake's emphasis on the happy-family aspect of the team reflects his personality. When he took over as coach following the St. Patrick's Day riot, he insisted on teamwork. As a player, Blake had been aggressive but not combative. He spent little time in the penalty box. He came to play hockey, not brawl. Because he had the instant respect of the players, including Richard, he brought the same attitudes to the team. A lot of time was spent with Richard, cooling off his temper, convincing him that no fight was worth the loss of a game and the Stanley Cup. Montreal's five consecutive championships began with the first day of Blake's coaching career. Newspapermen observed that under Blake the team was more closely knit. Rather than

A splendid surrealistic shot of Montreal's Guy Lafleur. Is that pensiveness or pride on his face? Or maybe fatigue or disgust? Or perhaps he's just counting up all those Stanley Cup earnings. (*Photo by Michel Ponomareff*)

Another save by the Montreal goalie.

cliques of players, as under Irvin, the whole Blake team was friendly. They played together on the ice and socialized as families off it.

Toe Blake on teamwork: "You must have the organization. The fans play an important role. But teamwork depends on the players. We were like a family. I never saw one of the players blackballed because his teammates didn't like him. Agreed, we let a lot of players go that didn't fit in. But very few players left that club with a bad word for their former teammates. Every kid in this province wants to play for the Canadiens. They all can't, of course, but when they do play elsewhere, most of them would rather be with the Canadiens. Yet I'll say this. You have to be lucky to keep an organization happy so long."

But Blake is speaking about the golden age of hockey. The current Canadiens are endeavoring to carry on in the tradition of the great teams of the past. And the Canadiens of today are good, with Captain Yvan Cournoyer, left wing Yvon Lambert, right wing Guy Lafleur, right wing Rejean Houle, defenseman Serge Savard, Jacques Lemaire, Pierre Bouchard, Guy Lapointe, Steve Shutt, Bob Gainey, and the others.

The only real question is how well this team compares with those of the past. Richard is openly scornful of modern hockey. He considers it a poor imitation of the past. The players don't skate as well, pass as well, use as much teamwork. They aren't even as tough in the bodychecks and brawls as those now retired. But the Canadiens remain the class of the league. As defenseman Serge Savard has put it, "Any way the other teams want to play the game, we can play that way, too." The Canadiens can skate a team off the ice, but if brawling it is to be, the team is prepared to play that game also. It would seem that the dynasty remains in excellent hands.

DALLAS COWBOYS

In this uncertain world, there are few things as predictable as the appearance of the Dallas Cowboys in the playoffs of the National Football League. Since 1965, the Cowboys have been in the playoffs every year save one, 1974. They have won the Super Bowl twice and appeared in two others. Even in losing, they have provided some of the monumental moments in the history of the sport. The Cowboys are truly dynastic. They have won and won despite many, many changes in personnel, although the ownership and coaching have remained constant. Despite all their winning, the team once had a "losers" tag placed on them. How they overcame this makes an inspirational story of teamwork.

Organizing to Win

I think confidence comes from the whole organization.
Tom Landry

The popularity of professional football in the United States
is no accident. A great deal of intelligent design went into
making it a dominant spectator sport.

The game itself was changed to accommodate television.
Historically, the game had featured two beefy, seven-man
lines grunting it out on the turf so a fellow in the backfield
could hopefully gain a few yards running the ball. Professional football changed that with the passing game. Strong-
armed quarterbacks could throw to five receivers, and only
the tight end was really a lineman. The split end was
moved away from the line, and a back, called a flanker,
was stationed far to the side. In variations of the T formation, the quarterback took the ball from under the center
and fell back to pass. The defense responded with the 4-3
formation—four bulky linemen up front, three linebackers
behind him, and four defensive backs to combat the passing

game. Some teams are now using a 3-4 defense—three linemen, four linebackers, and four defensive backs.

The effect was to open up the game for television. The ball was big enough to show up on home screens—no small problem for televised hockey—and the plays occurred over a large area of the field. There were lots of long plays, all easily seen, and plenty of bone-crunching tackles in the open field. Television viewers could see often better than the fans in the stands. Teams could score quickly, if not always easily, creating lots of high-scoring games decided in the final seconds. Professional football became a natural for television, and the National Football League obliged by providing various types of playoffs, culminating in the Super Bowl to decide which *one* team was best. Human beings like to have things decided with one ultimate victor who is declared champion. The NFL, unlike college football, offered that.

Something more important happened behind the scenes. In one of the most enlightened decisions ever reached in American sports, the owners of the NFL teams voted to share equally the television receipts. Consider it. Owners of teams in New York, Los Angeles, and Chicago, each with many millions of potential viewers, shared equally the television money with a team such as Green Bay, which could attract perhaps only hundreds of thousands of viewers. Share and share alike meant that each team in the league would be financially successful. Each team would have the money to afford good players. Professional baseball has never had this wisdom.

Then there is the player draft. The teams with the poorest records draft the best players each year. By drafting wisely, the weak teams could become strong in a few years. This happened. Green Bay, Miami, Pittsburgh, Dallas, Baltimore, and Minnesota were all cellar dwellers at one time.

The result is a situation—except perhaps in those years when expansion teams are added—in which any team is capable of beating any other on a given day. There are many upsets. Several teams are in contention, and Super Bowl champs are often decided by such factors as a lucky bounce of the ball or an absence of injuries. It is not an entirely idle fancy to imagine the situation one year in which all the teams in the league end up with identical 8–8 records, creating a playoff of monumental proportions. But then this probably won't happen, because there are ways for a team to get a slight edge on other teams. The ability to find this edge over a period of years is what accounts for the dynastic success of the Dallas Cowboys.

The team was formed in 1960 and lost every game that year. But this also-ran category was not to remain very long. Beginning with the 1965 season, the Cowboys have been in some form of playoff every year save 1974. Few teams have been such consistent winners. How do the Cowboys do it?

The name of the game in Dallas, the source of the competitive edge, is *organization*. From top to bottom, the Cowboys are the best-run team in the NFL. It begins with Clint Murchison, principal owner and chairman of the Board. He ranks as one of the richer, or maybe richest, men in the United States. He enjoys owning the team, participating in its activities, and bringing a winner to his hometown of Dallas. All of this qualifies him for the moniker of "wealthy sportsman."

Murchison has done something far more important, however: He has surrendered his ego to winning. More than a few sports teams have run into difficulties because the owner has become jealous of his general manager, coaches, and players. They receive the glory and publicity. People recognize them on the street, ask for autographs. It is not unusual for an owner to resent this and seek more of the spotlight for himself. Murchison has been more content to let others run the team while he participates behind the scenes. This has eliminated a lot of friction.

Murchison has also brought continuity to the Cowboys. Since the inception of the team there has been one general manager, Texas E. Schramm; one vice president of personnel development, Gil Brandt; and one coach, Tom Landry. Other key positions have been similarly filled. The team put together a good organization and stuck with it. A bad season occurs, or maybe just a disappointing one. The coach and general manager are not fired. The effort goes into finding what is lacking in the team and correcting the deficiency.

The Dallas Cowboys today have an experienced front office. This has a subtle yet important effect. The Cowboys came from nowhere to be consistent winners. Somebody upstairs must be doing something right. A great deal of confidence exists that the right players are being drafted, the right trades being made. Too, the knowledge that Murchison, Schramm, Brandt, and Landry are there to stay puts the players in the position of blaming themselves for a less than ideal season. It doesn't do any good to blame the front office or the coach for the failure. They have a proven record of success. The problem must lie elsewhere—with the players, the team.

In their search for that slight competitive edge, the Cowboys have perfected, as near as any such inexact science can be, methods for finding the players who make a winner. Schramm learned his football under Dan Reeves of the Los Angeles Rams. Reeves is in the Hall of Fame as an owner. He participated in and encouraged the decisions that made the NFL so successful. He was the first to bring major-

Win or lose, Coach Tom Landry of the Dallas Cowboys takes his work seriously, thereby gaining a reputation as sober and unsmiling. Landry also wins praise for his sartorial excellence.

league sports to the West Coast. He pioneered the modern system of football scouting.

Prior to Reeves, pro coaches used to draft and sign players on the basis of their newspaper clippings. Or perhaps they'd call up a few college coaches to solicit recommendations about good players on their teams or other teams they had played. It was all very informal, and the errors were monumental. Reeves was the first to hire scouts to search full time for talent. He sought to make player selection more scientific. For many years the Los Angeles Rams had the best talent of any team in the league.

Schramm came from Los Angeles and perfected Reeves' ideas at Dallas. The result is a storehouse of football talent that makes Dallas a consistent winner. That is no mean feat. Consider the problems. Every team is looking for the big, fast, aggressive player who knows how to play and has the desire to give 100 per cent to the demands of the game. Such people are rather rare. At least until other NFL teams copied the Dallas recruiting system, coaches felt there were seldom more than a dozen players a year, often fewer, who were ready to step from college into the pros. Teams could make their first draft picks, perhaps their second, but after that it was a case of pay your money and take your chances that the player would be useful.

Reeves, then Schramm, sought to find out how good these thousands of college players are. Reading the newspapers was often misleading. Each year, for example, the Heisman trophy is awarded to the best college player. The record of success of Heisman trophy winners in the NFL is not a particularly good one. There are several reasons for this. Many of the winners are quarterbacks, and that is a very special position in the pros. The pros require extraordinary talents, and there aren't more than two or three a decade who are standouts. At this very moment, half the teams in the NFL would dump their starting quarterbacks if they could just obtain a super guy.

Heisman trophy winners, and many of the other college standouts, run into difficulties in the pros because they are too small. College teams weigh a good bit less than professional teams. An outstanding college runner, for example, may not be able to make those five- and ten-yard gains against all those beefy guys in the pros. And the college scatback often finds that he cannot outrun and outfake the pros. Face it: The pros are a tiny fraction of the players, the biggest, fastest, most experienced, the living best. Even a top-notch college player has a tough time just making the team.

Then there is the matter of publicity. The bigger colleges employ full-time press staffs to grind out press releases on the local team and its stars. It brings the fans into the college stadiums. A college player can be quite famous, getting lots of press coverage. What the coverage often doesn't say is that those big gains on the ground came from top linemen who blocked for him; those passes were completed because of a talented receiver; those stunning statistics were racked up against weak opponents; those impressive performances came because the whole team was very good, while a single individual was nothing special.

Until recent years, pro scouts had a difficult job. They could read the programs, often containing lies about the size and weight and accomplishments of a player. They could watch him in a game situation. But what did they really know? They could hardly enter the locker room to measure his height, put him on the scale to weigh him, and get out their stopwatch to see how fast he ran forty yards in full football gear.

Even if accurate information about these basics is known, scouts can still be misled. Even the Cowboys, who have refined scouting to an "exact" science, make mistakes. Take David McDaniels. The Cowboys picked him as a second-round draft choice, surely an exalted position, in 1968. How could they miss? He was 6-4 and weighed 200 pounds, a wide receiver with speed and size. He showed up at camp and everyone began whipping themselves. Six-four? He had shrunk 2 inches. He was 200 pounds? Believe 185. Fleet of foot? He could barely keep up with the offensive tackles in the 40-yard dash. Yet the scouting report was there. He ran the 40 in 4.3 seconds, the fleetest of the fleet. How could such an undersized, slow-footed end have been drafted second? The Cowboys determined to find out. The answer: McDaniels' college had measured their yard markers incorrectly. McDaniels ran not 40 yards in 4.3 but 36 yards. Fortunately for the Cowboys, every team believed he ran the 40 in 4.3. He was dealt to the Philadelphia Eagles for Mike Ditka, an All-Pro end. The Eagles shipped him to the Bears, who traded him to the Rams, who dumped him on the New Orleans Saints. To suggest that every team has been misled in drafting players is to suggest the obvious.

Nor is it just a matter of physical ability. Mental attitude is important. Consider two cases. Raymond Berry in his day caught more passes for more yardage than anyone who ever played the game. Yet Berry was not very tall and weighed 185. He was legally blind without his glasses. One leg was shorter than the other and most linemen could beat him in a foot race. Yet Raymond Berry considered it an affront to God to drop a football. If John Unitas got it within a yard of him, glue-fingered Berry could catch it and hold onto it. Compare him to Joe Don Looney. Out of Oklahoma, he had everything as a running back—size, speed, instinct for the hole. But Joe Don, a nice fellow really, was flaky. He couldn't concentrate. He'd get down on himself and mad at everyone else. By temperament he was a roman candle. Team after team tried him. He bombed every time. Mental attitude can compensate for physical liabilities. How do you tell a Berry from a Looney? Is the player a prima donna? Or is he determined to win when the going gets tough? Can he take instruction? Does he possess those mysterious ingredients of guts, desire, and leadership that make a winner?

Another factor. Not all the football is played in the Big Ten, Southwest Conference, Big Eight, or the Pacific Coast Conference. There are lots of players who sweat it out for whatsis college, unsung, unknown, written up in the local weekly newspaper. Could some of these fellows be pro material? Maybe a small college will produce only one pro player every ten years, but wouldn't it be nice to know about him? Or how about the late bloomer? Maybe he grows two inches and puts on forty pounds during the summer after graduation. Maybe he never had a chance to play, yet has tremendous desire. He'd make a splendid pro defensive back or kick-return specialist. How do you find him?

In the 1960s, Dallas began to locate these fellows, or a lot of them. Schramm and Brandt hired a full-time scouting team. Brandt also began to ask former players, from whatever team, to report on sandlot players, semipro teams, high-school, and small-college players who just might make it. A philosophy developed. Look for the *best athlete*. Forget filling a particular position. He didn't even have to be a football player for the Cowboys to be interested. Baseball, track, basketball, and soccer players are great athletes. If a guy can run the 100 in 9.4 or jump the high hurdles or fake a guard out of his pants on the way to the basket or slide into second to break up the double play, he can with a little instruction learn to play football. A natural athlete can learn to play anything.

For example, some years ago in Spain I participated in a pickup softball game. On the opposing team was a shortstop named Lew Hoad, the Australian tennis champ. It was the first time he'd ever played baseball. But in that game Hoad, a natural athlete, looked like a combination Bert Campaneris in the field and Johnny Bench at the plate.

The Cowboys showed a genius for finding unsung players. Consider Jethro Pugh, drafted on the eleventh round from Elizabeth City Teachers College; or Rayfield Wright, from Fort Valley State; or Pettis Norman, from Johnson C. Smith College; or Cliff Harris, from Ouachita Baptist. And it isn't always the unknown school. Calvin Hill played for Yale. Everyone knows they don't play *real* football at Yale. The Cowboys didn't know that. Or take Roger Staubach. Everyone knew he was the Heisman trophy winner, but he was too small. Besides, he was a Navy career man. The Cowboys didn't know—or believe. Then there are basketball players Cornell Green, Ron Widby, and Pete Gent, and Austrian soccer star Toni Fritsch and trackman Mike Gaechter and, oh yes, the world's fastest human, Bob Hayes. Who would have thought he could learn to catch all those football bombs? The Cowboys thought maybe he could.

The Cowboys learned to search constantly for talent, visiting college after college, even touring Europe for soccer players, with tape measures and stopwatches in hand. No information on a player is ever insignificant. Nor does the information gather dust in a file. All of it is active in a computer. Come the draft, come the time to invite a non-drafted free agent for a tryout, the computer spews out the statistics that might find a valuable player.

So a prospect signs with another team, a highly desired

Roger Staubach, former Heisman trophy winner and peerless Dallas quarterback, doing what he does best.

draft pick gets away to the Giants, Chiefs, or Broncos. All is not lost. There are always trades. The Cowboys keep in the computer information on every active player. He may have talents not needed by the Oilers or Lions, but he might fill a current need for the Cowboys. He may be a bit hard to handle for the Packers or Cards, but with different treatment, he might just blossom in Dallas.

The Dallas scouting system is now used routinely throughout the National Football League. But Dallas, by working at it harder, still manages to find more than their share of talent. In their long dynasty, the Cowboys have never faded for long. They feed in a couple of players a year, replacing the old with the new. Other teams can blame this continuity of talent on the club's peerless organization.

Paradoxically, the Cowboys, possessing all this new talent, make it difficult for a rookie to crash the lineup. The team uses such complex offensive and defensive plays that even the brainiest and most dedicated player is years in learning it all. The genius behind the complexity is Coach Tom Landry, the only coach Dallas has ever had.

His tenure is in itself remarkable, for over his seventeen seasons he has presented Dallas fans with enough disappointments to bring the ax down on the heads of a half-dozen coaches. After all, the New York Yankees once fired Yogi Berra because he lost the World Series in seven games. But the Dallas management determined at the outset that Tom Landry was the best coach around. Murchison and Schramm stuck with him. Thus shielded by long-term contracts, Landry has compiled an overall record that cannot be denied, even if his critics think he should have done better.

Colorful is hardly the word to describe Landry. He rarely shows any emotion in winning or losing. He is famous for being unsmiling. If fans watch him in hopes of seeing displays of hand-wringing, stomping, and teeth-gnashing, they are bound to be disappointed. No Woody Hayes is Tom Landry. Yet over the years Landry's flat effect has become something of a legend. Beneath that apparent calmness lies a fierce competitive spirit. Winning is every bit as important to him as it was to Vince Lombardi who suggested that winning was the only thing. Landry simply believes that he is more likely to win if he remains in control of himself and conveys the impression to his players that he knows what he is doing. An even better reason is that Landry's system used by the Cowboys is so complex that it requires players to think all the time. There is little room in either his attack or his defense for that superemotional play that characterizes many football teams.

As an assistant coach with the New York Giants in the 1950s, Landry invented the 4-3 defense, which revolutionized football. That fact alone would rank him as one of the supreme tacticians in the history of the game.

When Landry came to Dallas he set about refining the 4-3. What he did in essence was to demand that each player violate his basic football instinct, which is to go for the ball. Instead, each player is to secure his designated area or complete his defensive assignment before going for the ball. Thus if a play appears to be going inside, the coordinated defense of the Cowboys may still require players to defend the outside. Landry's defensive teams were years in understanding his system and developing the self-discipline to perform it. During the early years of the franchise the Cowboys scored a great deal, but they gave up more points. Dallas began to be a winner in 1965, precisely because Landry's defensive teams began to use his system effectively. Ever since Dallas has fielded strong defensive teams. But it takes even the best rookie a couple of years to learn it.

The offensive unit faces similar problems. The Dallas playbook is fat. The players have to learn dozens of formations and practice until they can execute scores of assignments perfectly. Even with Landry and his staff calling all the plays from the sidelines, a Dallas quarterback is years learning the headwork before he becomes effective. It takes experience to play Landry's style of football.

Landry has been successful with his methods, yet a certain controversy underlies his coaching. The reverse of Landry's brainy complexity was the gutsy, basic football used by Vince Lombardi at Green Bay. Comparisons between the two coaches were natural. Both had been Giant assistant coaches, Landry for defense, Lombardi for offense. At Green Bay, Lombardi used fundamental football, overpowering opponents by running over and through them. This is not easy in the NFL, where everyone is big and tough. To win by pure strength and desire, Lombardi's players had to be psyched up to an emotional peak. Their adrenalin had to flow in buckets to enable them to perform the feats of strength and will that made them such a great team. Lombardi was a master at using intimidation and psychology to psych his players. The mark of a Lombardi team was the number of games they won by sheer will to win.

Some of the great games in professional football occurred when teams coached by these two dissimilar men met. Lombardi had gone to Green Bay in 1959 and won the NFL championship in 1961 and 1962. The Packers lost the next two years, then won again in 1965. Landry had gone to Dallas in 1960 and lost every game. The team gradually improved, and in 1965 it compiled a 7–7 record and went to something called the "Playoff Bowl" between the second-place teams of the two NFL conferences. Dallas lost to the Colts, 35–3, but held a celebration anyhow. Schramm and Landry knew this young Texas team had come of age.

They were right. In 1966, Dallas compiled a 10–3–1 record and was considered the new power in the league. It was the first year of the Super Bowl between the National and American Football leagues—which Schramm was instrumental in helping to arrange. Dallas almost made it, but lost the NFL title to Green Bay in a wide-open 34–27 game. Lombardi, not Landry, led his team to the first Super Bowl victory.

The next year, 1967, Dallas seemed the team to beat. But there were lots of injuries. Particularly hampered was quarterback Don Meredith, one of the great ones. He had had his great years when Dallas was weak. Now that the team was strong, he was hurting. Dallas won nine and lost five, then got it together to demolish Cleveland, 52–14, for the Eastern Conference title. That set up a rematch with Green Bay for the NFL title and a trip to Super Bowl II.

The game was a football classic, much remembered to this day. It was played in late December in Green Bay. It was bitter cold. The field was frozen, and the fingers of the players not much better. The runners couldn't run, the passers pass, or the receivers catch. The players dubbed it the "Ice Bowl." The game was a defensive struggle. Green Bay led, 10–7, at the half. Dallas came out, well briefed by Landry. More importantly, a slit had been cut in the front of Meredith's jersey so he could warm his hands between plays. Dallas scored. It was 14–10 Dallas until late in the game. Then Green Bay got a drive going. With less than half a minute to play, Green Bay had a first down on the Dallas one-yard line.

It was the reverse of the previous year. Then, behind by a touchdown, Dallas had been on the Green Bay one-yard

He's now a broadcaster and actor, but may it not be forgotten what a splendid quarterback ''Dandy'' Don Meredith was for the Dallas Cowboys.

line with seconds remaining. Dallas had failed to score. Now, needing a touchdown to win, Green Bay attacked the Dallas line and failed. Time out was called. Again Green Bay ran at the Cowboys. Again Dallas held, and again time was called. There was time for only one play. Green Bay elected for a touchdown and victory, not a field goal and a tie. Quarterback Bart Starr kept the football on a quarterback sneak, not risking a handoff to frigid fingers or a lost footing on the frozen sod. Behind a superhuman block by offensive guard Jerry Kramer—it made him a celebrity— Starr fell into the end zone. It was a bitter, bitter loss for Dallas.

Landry: "In the first championship game against Green Bay we lost to one of the great teams of all time. In the second, we felt we were a better team. But those old Green Bay veterans, so very experienced, managed to squeak by us. It was a great blow and we were presented with a most difficult morale problem."

Indeed. Those two last-second losses to Green Bay made Dallas "the team that couldn't win the big ones." For the next several seasons, the Cowboys, with a truly great team did nothing to discourage the reputation. In 1968, the team compiled a 12–2 record, then lost the Eastern Conference playoff to Cleveland, 31–20. In 1969, they devoured regular-season opponents, 11–2–1, then played dead to Cleveland again, 38–14. In 1970, the team went 9–5, squeaked by Detroit, 5–0 (if such a score is to be believed), and San Francisco, then lost the Super Bowl to Baltimore, 16–13 —with another last-second field goal.

Yet statistics don't tell the tale of that season. The team came of age that year. Dallas beat Philadelphia and the New York Giants to begin the season, lost to St. Louis, shut out Atlanta, then was stomped by Minnesota, 54–13. They beat Kansas City and edged by Philadelphia. It was hardly a record to inspire confidence. That great football team in Texas was clearly on the ropes, shackled with a can't-win-the-big-ones reputation, broken in spirit, rife with dissension. There were cries for Landry's head.

Those woes were followed by disaster. On "Monday Night Football," before a national television audience, Dallas was shellacked by St. Louis, 38–0. Landry: "The Cardinals just killed us. Everybody wrote us off. We had a 5–4 record and couldn't beat any of the good teams. But that game made us. It showed we had character, as I always knew we did. We came off the floor and began to win. It would have been easy to quit, but we didn't. We won every game after that until the Colts beat us with that field goal."

Then in 1971 Dallas buried the can't-win reputation forever. They won eleven and lost three against tough opponents, then beat Minnesota, San Francisco, and Miami to become Super Bowl champs.

For those who like happy endings, there is a certain justice in those two seasons. The Colts, having suffered bitter disappointments, won the Super Bowl from Dallas with an aging team past its prime. Pure determination carried the day. The next year Dallas returned to wash away all its past defeats with a victory over a splendid Miami Dolphin team. Miami, of course, returned to win two consecutive Super Bowls.

The can't-win moniker pinned to Dallas was always unfair. In the higher reaches of league play, eight, then four, and finally the two best teams vie for ultimate victory. Each wants to win as badly as the other. Yet one team must lose. Dallas came as close to victory as possible. They lost repeatedly in the waning seconds on field goals and in goal-line stands. To pin a can't-win tag on them was cruel. The same label could have been applied at various times to the

Colts, Rams, Vikings, Raiders, Chiefs, Redskins, 49ers, and Browns. But it was the Cowboys who were given the reputation. They had to live with it. That they overcame it is a tribute to the Cowboys as a team. In his interview, Landry said he was more proud of that than any of the Dallas victories. Who will disagree?

As you talk to the Cowboys about their team, you get a different message than you do from the Colt players, for example. With the Colts, the word is Unitas, then Bert Jones. Their great quarterbacks were the team leaders, the reason for their success. In Dallas the name most often mentioned is Tom Landry.

The Cowboys have had great quarterbacks, as every winning team must. Don Meredith, then Craig Morton, and finally Roger Staubach must be listed on the roster of the finest quarterbacks the game has known. Dallas players have high regard for them. Yet they have the status of just another player who contributes to the team. The reverence accorded Unitas is missing. This may be due to the fact that Landry calls the plays. He and his assistants are the strategists. Staubach executes the plays.

How does Landry make the Cowboys go as a team? There is some conflict of views. Landry: "I believe teamwork begins with the selection of personnel. I feel character is important to success, and character is built through adversity. A person can either surmount the adversity to become a champion, or he can turn to drugs and alcohol to escape. With character a person can pick himself up off the floor and go on to win.

"We have not had too many prima donnas on our team. We get some from time to time. They have great desire for individual success, but limited understanding of the team concept. We have been able to handle a few such people because of the makeup of the rest of the team. We have a nucleus of dedicated, committed people who can persevere to recover from a low point."

How is the nucleus of such people formed? Landry: "I believe it has to do with their level of confidence. When players first come to us they are so inexperienced in what makes a good team. We look for ways to show it to them. We try to find ways for them to measure what they can do, to measure what they can have confidence in—and to find out what price they must pay for success. Too, I think confidence comes from the whole organization. We have stability here in the management and coaching. We have a record of success. I think that experience lends confidence to the players. We try to maintain the nucleus by feeding a few new players in at a time. We have made some good trades. I've seen players change radically when they come with our organization. But mostly we try to build through the draft, bringing younger players along in our methods and inserting them in the lineup so their confidence grows. If you keep playing the same people, as Green Bay did, they are going to get old all at once and you find yourself out of contention."

A somewhat dissimilar view of the Cowboy success comes from Bob Lilly, the longtime Dallas All-Pro defensive lineman: "Our success begins with the organization. The owner has been interested but has not interfered with the scouting or coaching. Tex Schramm has been shrewd in making trades and scouting and keeping everything running. I think Landry learned a lot when Green Bay went down the well. You can't let a team get too old. You have to maintain the team with draft choices.

"As far as coaching goes, Landry is very innovative. His ideas are just a little more advanced than that of most coaches. His system is difficult to learn. It tends to weed out players who lack the desire or intelligence to master the

In his heyday, tackle Bob Lilly of Dallas was considered so tough that he didn't need a helmet.

system. To play for the Cowboys you must have great desire. You must be willing to put in extra study.

"Landry is innovative in training. Every year he comes up with something to make it interesting. It may be a weight program or a running program or something to make you think. There is always something added. It creates an atmosphere that something different is happening. There is lots of enthusiasm. He gets a lot of work from everybody. It is never the same old routine.

"I think, also, that Landry creates the correct atmosphere that makes us a team. It involves a lot of things—the uniforms, the fans, the stadium. You want to be a Cowboy. You are isolated from your friends and family. The work is real tough. You must make a total commitment to football. So you are working your tail off. So is everyone else. Everybody must win his position all over again each year. But the result of it is pride, pride in yourself, pride in the team."

Lilly spoke of Roger Staubach as a team leader in the sense of working very hard. But since he does not call the plays, he is not a leader as quarterbacks are on other teams. Lilly: "The Cowboys are a product of Landry."

How does he motivate the team? Landry: "I try to use praise as a motivation as much as possible. I think it works best, although fear as a motivation is used to some extent." Cliff Harris, outstanding eight-year defensive back for the Cowboys: "Landry is a great motivator, all right. But he is extremely subtle. He discusses with us what needs to be done. There is no rah-rah about it. He quietly explains the jobs we are to do. He simplifies it. He brings reality to what we are to accomplish."

Lilly's view is a bit different. It conflicts with the usual public image of Landry as a quiet, pious Christian gentleman. Lilly: "Landry uses fear motivation, pure and simple.

That fluid motion and the expression on his face show why perennial All-Pro safety Cliff Harris is one of the most feared defensive players in the league.

The million-dollar legs of Tony Dorsett during his outstanding rookie year for the Cowboys. In Texas, the former University of Pittsburgh star earned every penny.

RAYBESTOS BRAKETTES

A girls' softball team? Ranked with the Yankees, Celtics, Bruins, Canadiens, and other great teams? You gotta be kidding.

Not hardly. For starters, softball ranks as a major sport. Attendance at individual games may not be as high as in professional sports, but softball is without doubt the major team-participation sport in the United States. There are thousands of teams, both fast- and slow-pitch, male and female, organized into church, industrial, school, and other types of leagues. State, regional, national, and even international championships are held.

And if anyone, wallowing in ignorance, believes softball is a sissy sport suitable for middle-aged has-beens, he or she ought to try it. The ball may be a little larger, but it isn't soft. And the ground for that slide into home plate is just as hard. But if doubts remain, just try standing up at the plate and hitting a ball zooming at you eighty or ninety miles an hour from forty feet away. That is routine in softball—girls' softball, that is.

Perhaps the final word ought to come from Ralph Raymond, coach of the Raybestos Brakettes. "We used to play male teams for the competition and experience. But we quit that several years ago. When the male loses to girls, his ego gets bruised. He gets mad and starts some rough stuff. We decided the male ego wasn't worth having our players hurt."

The Raybestos Brakettes are a softball dynasty. They may be the best-known American sports team worldwide. It's a cinch the Brakettes are better known abroad than the Yankees, Celtics, or any football team. The Brakettes are authentic world champions. They won that title in 1974, winning nine straight games against the finest teams in the world. They won the world title in 1978 in El Salvador.

The Brakettes have won, as of the 1977 season, seven national championships in a row, twelve of fourteen, fourteen of twenty since 1958. And five other years they were runner-up to the national champs. The Brakettes, and all the other members of the American Softball Association, are amateurs, which leads to perhaps the most startling achievement in all of sports. After the 1975 season and five national titles, virtually the entire Brakettes team joined the new women's professional softball league. The Brakettes recruited a whole new team of young players and kept on winning in 1976 and 1977. Surely this remarkable dynasty can tell us more than a little about teamwork.

The Will to Win

Suck up your guts and go do it.
                                    Ralph Raymond

Kathy Strahan is twenty-one years old, 5-7, 130 pounds, and whistle bait. She is also the proverbial vacuum cleaner at either shortstop or second base.

"I think I was born with a ball in my hand. About my earliest memories are of playing catch with my dad in the backyard. I just always played, wanted to play, and enjoyed playing. You see, I was the oldest and I guess Dad didn't know what else was coming, so he set out to make a ball-player of me. I have two brothers, but neither is particularly interested in athletics."

When Kathy was fourteen, she started playing softball with the Lansing, Michigan, Laurels, a major team. But that was only in the summer, and she wanted to extend the season. In her senior year, she tried out for the varsity at

Lansing Hill High School—the boys' varsity baseball team. She won the starting second-base position.

"That was a first in the state of Michigan and a lot of people didn't like it. Particularly at local games, I'd get roundly booed every time I appeared on the field. Of course, all that has changed now, and girls can play on boys' teams."

Kathy says she had no particular trouble on the team. She was upset by the booing, but fortunately the baseball coach also taught psychology and was able to help her through a difficult period.

Kathy graduated from Michigan State in 1978 with a degree in physical education. She played second for the university women's team, which won the College World Series in 1976 and finished third in both 1975 and 1977. She plans to teach and coach and is already gaining experience as assistant girls basketball coach at her high-school alma mater.

Kathy also plays shortstop for the Raybestos Brakettes. She was spotted by Coach Ralph Raymond in 1975 playing for the Laurels. When his whole team turned pro, he asked her to join the Brakettes. Since that is the finest, most celebrated girls' softball team in the world, she jumped at the chance. "Coach Raymond immediately moved me to shortstop. I'd always played second. At first it was strange, the different angles and all, but now I love it." I asked her batting average. "I really don't know, but it was something over .300 last year, I think." It can't be said she or the other Brakettes compute their batting averages on the way to first base.

The Brakettes are the finest women's softball team ever put together and without doubt one of the great teams of all time in any sport. They are reigning world champions and the perennial national champs. In softball, they are a

The legendary Joan Joyce shows the form that made her the terror of women's softball. Her pitches were clocked at over 100 miles per hour.

Happy are the victors. Diane Schumacher (left) and Barbara Reinalda hug William S. Simpson, sponsor of the Raybestos Brakettes, following the winning game of the 1977 national championship.

household word. They play a tough seventy-to-eighty-game schedule, topped off by the grueling national championships against the top teams in the country. In this rarefied competition, the games are invariably low-scoring. A typical struggle may go fifteen or twenty innings and end up 1–0. It becomes a contest not so much of talent as of will and desire. "The game goes to the team that wants it more," Raymond says. And in games like this, don't wager any funds against the Brakettes. They are winners.

The Brakettes are an amateur team. The girls do it for fun, experience, and the opportunity it brings them. The list of former Brakettes who are coaches, athletic directors, and outstanding athletes is a long one. Perhaps the most celebrated is pitcher Joan Joyce, a living legend. She is now a member of the women's pro golf tour. The girls' expenses are paid and they have an opportunity for full- or part-time employment with the sponsoring Raybestos-Manhattan, Inc., headquartered in Trumbull, Connecticut. Even without paying the players a salary, Raybestos picks up a sizable tab. The Brakettes travel extensively, including trips to Japan, Australia, Europe, and South America. The traveling group consists of twenty people, fifteen players, as well as coaches and trainers. Since the team always goes first class, staying in the finest hotels and dining in posh restaurants, the tab for a week's tour of California or wherever is significant. When William S. Simpson, Raybestos official and softball enthusiast, formed the team in 1947, it was called the All-Stars. The next year the name was changed to the Brakettes. Raybestos manufactures automobile brake linings. A little advertising is probably only fair, considering all those hotel bills.

Even more than in hardball, the name of the game in softball is pitching. A good hard thrower of strikes is mandatory in major-league softball, and over the years the

Brakettes have had some super pitchers. Indeed, the great days of the Brakettes began when the two greatest pitchers the game has ever known joined the team. The senior member was Bertha Reagan Tickey. She literally learned to play with the boys, first with her brothers in her native California and then with boys' teams. At age thirteen she joined the Orange, California, Lionettes, the dominant team of the 1950s and longtime rival of the Brakettes. She helped pitch the Lionettes to their first national title in 1950. After winning five world championships in seven years, the Lionettes lost their sponsor. Bertha Tickey, considered the nation's No. 1 pitcher, was persuaded by Bill Simpson to come East to join the Brakettes.

That year 1956 marked the debut of a sixteen-year-old pitcher named Joan Joyce. The two were to make history. In that first year as teammates, they pitched the Brakettes into the national tournament in Clearwater, Florida. They didn't win the title that year, but Bertha Tickey was named the Most Valuable Player in the tourney, pitching six games before losing in the semifinals, 1–0, in seventeen innings. The next year the Brakettes were shut out in the first two games of the national tourney, 1–0 in both games. It would be some time before that happened again.

In 1958, the Brakettes won their first national championship. They won six straight on their way to the title. Tickey pitched four victories, three of them in extra innings. Joan Joyce pitched a no-hit, no-run game for a 2–0 victory. In the championship game against defending champions from Fresno, California, Tickey again took the mound. In the third inning, she collapsed from fatigue and was replaced by Joyce, who threw no-hit ball the rest of the way. The Brakettes won, 1–0, on a dramatic seventh-inning home run by Mary Hartman. The next two seasons were in

It's a trifle posed, but it is still a good shot of the celebrated Bertha Tickey
of the Brakettes, one of the great hurlers of all time.

the same pattern, with the Brakettes winning all six games for the championships, four by Tickey, two by Joyce.

The 1961 season was a heartbreaker for the Brakettes. Their string of eighteen consecutive world tourney victories was snapped on opening night by a 2–1 loss to Reading, Pennsylvania. But it takes two losses to eliminate a team from the tourney, and the second loss would be a while in coming. The Brakettes ran off eight straight victories to enter the championship game against the Gold Sox of Whittier, California, a team they had already beaten once. The game went an incredible nineteen innings as a 1–1 tie, although the Brakettes outhit the Sox, 9–5. The Brakettes left eighteen runners stranded. Then, in the bottom of the nineteenth, the Sox squeezed home a run from third. The loss ended Joyce's string of thirty-six straight wins over two seasons. In her losing nineteen-inning effort, she only struck out a mere forty.

The Brakettes returned as world champions in 1963, sweeping all six tournament games. Joyce won four, allowing only one earned run in thirty-four innings and striking out sixty-six. Bertha Tickey pitched two shutout victories, one of them a no-hitter. At the end of that season, Joanie Joyce decided to attend Chapman College in California. She left the Brakettes and joined the archrival Orange Lionettes. The confrontations between Joan and her old teammates were monumental. In 1964, Joyce pitched a no-hit, no-run game against the Brakettes on Opening Night, sending them into the losers' bracket. But the Connecticut girls were not yet out. They still had Ms. Tickey. She pitched fifty consecutive scoreless innings, including a victory over Orange, before giving up a run in the fourth inning of the finals against Portland, Oregon. That run held up to make the Brakettes runners-up.

The next year, 1965, Ms. Tickey pitched two no-hit, no-run games in the national tourney, setting the stage for the Brakettes-Lionettes confrontation in the finals. It was Joanie Joyce against Donna LoPiano. They dueled for twelve scoreless innings before the Lionettes pushed across a run to give Joyce the victory.

The next year the tables were turned. The Brakettes came out of the losers' bracket to dump Joyce and Orange twice on the way to the championship. The Brakettes had an incredible seventy-four wins against four losses that year. Ms. Joyce apparently decided that if she couldn't beat her former teammates, she might as well join them. Her return to Connecticut for the 1967 season made the team a force to be reckoned with. The Brakettes ran up a 67–2 record, including forty-three straight. They won everything in sight, including all six national tournament games. They weren't even scored upon. The pitching statistics were incredible that year. Donna LoPiano was 21–0, Joyce 19–0, Tickey 17–1, and Donna Hebert 10–1. And they did more than pitch. Joyce won the batting title with a .435 average, and LoPiano set a home-run record at eight. Both LoPiano and Tickey were named to the All-Star team as pitchers, leaving Joyce to be named as first baseperson. That season supposedly marked the retirement of Bertha Tickey. She pitched a no-hit, no-run game in the tourney, winning, 10–0, and decided to hang up her spikes.

But not for long. The next season Donna LoPiano went off to graduate school in California, and Donna Hebert underwent surgery. Tickey came out of retirement to help Joyce lead the Brakettes to still another title. That truly was Bertha Tickey's last season. She was in her mid-forties and a grandmother. All she did was notch a 25–1 record for the season. In the national tournament, she pitched two perfect games, the last one going thirteen innings. And who says women are the weaker sex?

Without Tickey, but with Donna LoPiano back on the club, the Brakettes were runners-up in 1969 and 1970. Then, starting in 1971, they began a string of national championships that has not ended through the 1978 season. The accomplishments over this period are little short of unbelievable. In 1971, the team went undefeated in 57 straight games. Joyce was 25–0, LoPiano 21–0, and Diane Warriner 11–0. In 1973, with the tournament held at the Brakettes' home field in Stratford, the team came out of the losers' bracket to win the championship. In 9 games, 69⅔ innings, Joyce gave up a single earned run. The string including 2 no-hit, no-run games. Over the entire season she won 37 games, pitched 132 consecutive scoreless innings, and recorded 34 shutouts, including 11 no-hit, no-run games. In addition, she had 83 hits for a .406 average and knocked in 55 runs. Superstar? And then some.

In 1974, the Brakettes represented the United States in the international tournament, sweeping all nine games. Joyce whipped the Australians twice, once with a no-hitter, the other with a perfect game, then one-hitted defending champion Japan for the title. In all, she pitched five shutouts in international competition.

A week later a tired Brakettes team was in Orlando, Florida, for the national tournament. They won the first two, then dropped a 2–1 game to Indianapolis. To retain their title, they now had to win seven in a row. They won the next five, three of them by 1–0 scores. The showdown came in a doubleheader against the Sun City Saints. Joyce, who had pitched twenty innings the night before, came back to win both halves of the doubleheader by 1–0 scores. The first game went fifteen innings, the second ten. Her status as the greatest women's softball pitcher of all time is not based on press clippings.

Coach Raymond says of Joyce and Tickey: "Pitching is

uppermost in softball and I was very fortunate to have the two best pitchers the game has ever known. Both ladies deserve all the accolades they have received. Joyce simply overpowered the hitters. She claims her fast ball was clocked at 115 miles an hour. I personally doubt that, but I'm sure it was a good 90 miles an hour. Tickey wasn't as fast as Joyce, but she had more savvy. She knew the hitters and kept book on them. She knew what they could hit and couldn't hit, and she'd put that ball right where they didn't want it. That ability was invaluable to her. I once saw her walk two batters to get to one she knew she could get out. And she did."

Despite their great pitching, the Brakettes clearly had something else. All those extra-inning, 1–0 games indicate, first, that there is a lot of good pitching around, and second, that pitching is purely defensive. It keeps the opponents from scoring, but it doesn't win the game.

A typical rally in the higher reaches of softball is maybe a walk or an error, a couple of sacrifices, and a squeeze bunt for the score. A double, a sacrifice, and a fly ball have won many a softball game. The ability to do this, while keeping opponents from executing the same stratagems, is the hallmark of the Brakettes. Consider what it takes to win games like this. Superior pitching and flawless defense, to be sure. But over fifteen or twenty innings, it also takes endless patience, incredible poise, and iron-willed determination not to be beaten and to prevail. These qualities are not taught. Where do they come from?

Raymond: "I think it begins with the sponsor. Raybestos has been a top-flight sponsor. Simpson is genuinely interested in the game and wants to do anything to make the team a winner. For example, we now play the type of schedule guaranteed to make us get better. If we played only local teams, we'd never improve. But we play the best

Long hair flying, the Brakettes' Sue Enquist hits the dirt in a head-first dive for the plate. She beat the tag and was safe.

teams in the country—indeed, in the world. Our sponsor backs us for all the travel. And we go first class. The girls don't have to raise money with bake sales and raffles. They can concentrate on softball. And playing top-flight teams has enabled us to get better and better.

"Because we are the best and most famous team, lots of girls want to play for us. They come for tryouts and we pick the best. Even if we can't use them now, we keep tabs on them for the future. I look for five things—in order—in building a team: pitching, sound defense, speed, attitude, and hitting. You can always teach a player to hit fairly well. In championship play scores are low and hitting isn't that important."

What attitude? "I look for players with plenty of heart, plenty of guts. And I want them to be willing to work hard. And they do work hard. Coaching women's sports is a throwback to the old days. Women are much more committed than men. I coach high-school football and I've coached a lot of high-school and college baseball. I treat these girls exactly as I would male players. I use the same conditioning, the same emphasis on fundamentals of play. And they react to it and come back for more. If I said to my high-school team that there would be no practice Monday through Thursday and we'd get ready on Friday for a Saturday game, that would be all right with them. If I said that to these girls, they'd get together and hold their own practice. If I called a practice at three o'clock in the morning, they'd all show up. They work hard. They demand a lot from themselves. That's why they are so successful."

That is doubtless a factor, but there is more to the Brakettes' dynasty. Bertha Tickey: "The secret to the Brakettes is coaching and teamwork. I played under other male coaches, and Ralph Raymond is the best there is. He handles the girls exactly as he would a men's team. Quite a few other male coaches I played under can't quite forget that girls are girls. They have a tendency to treat them as girls. They can't do any better or they can't try harder—that sort of thing. They don't push the girls as hard as Raymond does. And he is an excellent teacher. There are very few natural athletes anymore. People have to be taught. Raymond works on sliding and bunting and fielding. He teaches them what to do and makes them practice until they get it right. The girls react to this teaching and to the demands he makes upon them."

Raymond: "My idols as coaches are Vince Lombardi of the Packers and Walter Alston of the Dodgers. I know those are opposites. Lombardi was a tough, demanding, must-win coach, and Alston was the quiet man, rather fatherly. In girls' softball, that's the way you have to be. You need both of these qualities."

Kathy Strahan: "I used to believe that the more talent you have, the less coaching you need. When I came to the Brakettes I found this wasn't the case. The Brakettes have lots of talent, but they don't have all the outstanding talent. The difference is coaching. Mr. Raymond coaches like Vince Lombardi. He is tough. He demands 100 per cent all the time. He knows we can do it and we can do it better. He expects so much out of us. When I don't live up to his expectations, I feel badly, and I push myself harder to please him."

Kathy Strahan again: "The Brakettes have a lot of pride. We're No. 1. We're the best there is. There is a long tradition of being the best, and Mr. Raymond expects us to live up to it. He talked to us the last season about what he called the Three C's. The first was Cause. Our cause was winning the national championship again and earning the right to go to the international championships in Tokyo.

The second C is Courage, and the third is Confidence. Cause, Courage, and Confidence. He expected us to have that. He said he'd back us 150 per cent in anything we do. Now, how are you going to let down a man like that? I'll do anything for him."

Does Raymond really treat women players the same as men? Well, not quite. Raymond: "I do very little different with girls than boys as far as exercise, running, throwing, that sort of thing. Oh I try to do it in such a way as not to be abusive. I use no foul language, for example. If there is one big difference between girl athletes and boys, it is in the area of emotion. If a young lady has a tough time, maybe she is not hitting or makes a bad play, she has a tendency to cry a little. A male in the same situation feels bad, maybe gets down in the dumps, but he bounces back. Girls often take losses a little harder. When this happens, my job is to sell. I have a chat with the girl. I try to buck her up, make her understand the season is seventy or eighty games long and she'll do better next time. I have to be a bit of a psychologist, and I think I've had excellent success at it. I do a little bit of everything. There's a time to chew them out and a time to praise. I suppose I do a trifle more fathering of girls than boys, but they know when I'm mad and disappointed."

Kathy Strahan: "I don't cry myself. I hold it all in. But I have seen it. There are some tears in the dugout. A girl makes an error at a crucial point in the game. She feels terrible. She's let down the whole team. She lets her emotions out in the form of tears. But it usually doesn't incapacitate her. She has a cry, then goes back in and tries harder. Occasionally, though, someone will get so emotionally upset she is just going to mess up everything and make it worse. At that point, Mr. Raymond takes her out and sets her on the bench to work it out herself.

"After coming to the Brakettes, I realized I'd rather play under a male coach than a woman. Women do tend to be more emotional, and I think a woman coach understands that and relates to it too much. She can feel what is happening to the player, and she tends to hang in there with her to let her deal with it. And if she doesn't deal with it very well, the woman coach tends to become irritated. They maybe both get into an emotional high and there is real trouble. They have words and maybe don't speak to each other the rest of the season. A male coach is better, I think, because he doesn't understand these problems and doesn't try to deal with them. He expects the player to cope with her emotions. If she doesn't he takes her out and sets her on the bench. It's much better to ignore these things, really it is."

Raymond: "I have certain key words I use in talking to these young ladies. I use words like 'heart' and 'guts' and 'poise' and 'pride.' I tell them to suck up your guts and go do it. But the most important word I use is *family*.' I'm a family man. I have seven children and we're all close. I believe that the family that plays together and works hard together will get the job done. The Brakettes are a family. We work hard together, we play together, and we pull together. There is no dissension on the team. Oh I guess maybe there was a little jealousy when I first came with the club in 1966, but I got rid of the troublemakers. These girls all like each other and they know the whole team is as good as the weakest player. And all the Brakettes have families who support them. They come to the games and root for them. That's important."

Kathy Strahan: "All the girls on the team are talented, and no one is above the other. Sure pitching is important, but it takes other players on the field. On her best day,

Joanie Joyce couldn't win without good players behind her, and she knew it. She didn't consider herself better than anyone else."

Raymond consistently refers to his players as "young ladies," a term that is a no-no in the higher reaches of women's liberation. I asked him if he had trouble with women's lib. He replied, "No, not really. Oh maybe there was a little problem with Joanie Joyce her last year. She was getting together with Billie Jean King to form the professional softball league. But it didn't amount to much. I can't say women's lib has been a problem for me." That may be because he treats his players no differently than male athletes. Besides, the act of being a woman player means they are already quite liberated. Sliding into home plate in short pants hardly equates with playing with dolls.

The crisis for the Brakettes came at the end of the 1975 season, when virtually the entire team joined the pro circuit. Only three players stayed with the team, and only one of those, outfielder Beth Quesnel, had been a starter. Her story:

"I played boys' Little League when I was twelve, but I never got to play after that. I lived in Maine and there weren't any teams there. I started to play regularly when I was twenty-four or twenty-five and moved to Mystic, Connecticut, in 1971. I tried out for the Brakettes, but I wasn't good enough. So I played with the Bridgeport, Connecticut, Co-eds. They played in the same league as the Brakettes. Then in 1975 I had improved enough so I was invited to join the Brakettes. It was Joyce's last year and I rode the bench a lot. That team had everything, super pitching, super defense. The hitting came at will. With the pitching and defense, we were always in the ball game, so a couple of hits would win it.

Gently, gently. Never in women's softball, as Beth Quesnel of the Brakettes found out as she was tagged out at the plate by Maru Hutton of Washington.

"After that season, Mr. Simpson and Coach Raymond put together a whole new team. They picked up a super pitcher and they found the best athletes they could. That was the secret. We're all good, all-around athletes. We all play other sports. Then we worked real hard on defense. And we had the Brakettes' pride. We kept on winning."

Raymond's version: "You have to understand that the Brakettes are the best. Everybody wants to play for us. Over the years a lot of young ladies had tried out for us. They were good, but there wasn't room for them. Suddenly in 1976 there was lots of room. I remembered these youngsters who had tried out earlier and invited them to try out again. We now have a very young team. Four girls are only fifteen, two are sixteen, and two are seventeen. No one other than Beth Quesnel is over twenty-five. We worked very hard to make a team. And in 1976 we lost a lot of games for the Brakettes. Our record was 37–11. But the girls didn't give up on themselves. They hung in there, practiced hard, and improved. We swept the national tournament in seven games. In 1977, we had to come out of the losers' bracket to win, beating out the Ashland, Ohio, Sabres for the title. What a game that was. Twice Ashland had runners on third with nobody out and they never scored. We got one of them with a play at the plate. Lisa Brummel was catching, and there was absolutely no way she was going to let that run cross the plate. It was marvelous."

The key to the rebuilding process was a tip from a Raybestos salesman on the West Coast. He had spotted a young junior-college pitcher, Barbara Reinalda, just twenty years old. Raymond took one look at her and knew he was seeing "the new Joanie Joyce." She is a tall blonde with a big grin and a cherubic face. She resembles a large, econ-

omy-sized Hayley Mills. And she throws hard. In her first
season, she pitched all seven games of the national tournament, allowing only three earned runs in fifty-one innings.
The Brakettes' dynasty seems to be in good hands.

A game of inches, as the Brakettes' Sue Enquist finds out as she misses
this bunt attempt during 1977 play.

OAKLAND A'S

Admittedly, my choice of the Oakland A's for this book is a study in inconsistency and illogic. Having written about the New York Yankees, I should have chosen a National League team as the second baseball entry. The logical choice is the Los Angeles Dodgers, formerly of Brooklyn. That team has been a contender so often on both coasts that it is truly dynastic. Only my determination not to use two teams from Los Angeles keeps the Dodgers out of this book. A second logical choice is the Cincinnati Reds. A powerhouse team, surely, the Reds are not here because theirs has been basically one team. More, I didn't want to choose two teams from Ohio. Living in Ohio, I'd be accused of favoritism.

But why, in heaven's name, the Oakland A's? That's a second team from California. It is a second American League team. There is nothing dynastic about the A's. They were a good team, winning three world championships in a row. But it was a single team. Why the A's, for pity sakes?

Because this is a book about teamwork and how it is

achieved. The A's were the antithesis of much that has been written in these pages. We've read a lot herein about the importance of selecting the right players of a certain character, of the importance of a benevolent front-office organization, of the players being one big happy family. The A's had none of that. They had the opposite. Yet the A's were the dominant team in baseball in the early 1970s. What made them a great team?

The Madder They Got

There'd be an argument and then a fight, but after that
it was all baseball.

Catfish Hunter

Jim "Catfish" Hunter, now with the Yankees, recalls an incident when he was the star pitcher for the Oakland A's:

"It was just before the first World Series game in Los Angeles in 1972. I arrived at the clubhouse ahead of the rest of the team, which was coming by bus. When I got there, Ken Holtzman was talking to a member of the L.A. clubhouse staff. This fellow asked Holtzman if all the stories were true about the fighting on the team. Or was it just a lot of stuff made up by the press? Holtzman assured him the press only knew half of it. Just then the rest of the team entered the locker room. Blue Moon Odom and Rollie Fingers were arguing. Soon they were swinging at each other. The rest of us broke it up, but not until Odom was on the floor with blood all over his face. We hustled him to a doctor and it took six stitches to close the cut on his head. Odom was supposed to start the game, and he did and we won. Fingers relieved Odom and then I came in to relieve Rollie late in the game."

This incident hardly conjures up an image of the successful baseball team. Here are the A's players achieving the dream of a lifetime, playing in their first World Series. Just before the game, the starting pitcher and the ace reliever bloody each other in a fist fight. It boggles the mind. In fact, there is very little about the Oakland A's that isn't mind-boggling. The players openly quarreled with each other. Dissension was a way of life on the club. Relief pitchers scoffed at starting pitchers for not finishing a game. Players regularly held out for higher salaries, then held a press conference to explain how unhappy they were when they didn't get more money and how much they wanted to be traded. The "Angry A's" they were called, and the appellation was only half the measure of the fact.

Yet they won three world championships in a row. They dominated the American League West for another three years. If winning is the criterion for a great team—is there any other?—then the Angry A's were a phenomenal team. But how did this squabbling bunch do it?

One of those who has an answer is Dal Maxvill. He had had ten good years with the St. Louis Cardinals. Then, when his talents had waned a bit, he was picked up by the A's as a utility infielder. He was with the team during their championship years. His answer to why Oakland won: "Talent. Winners have more ability, and that's why they win. It is talent that wins, not fans, not coaches, not owners or anything else. The A's were a bunch of very good ballplayers, and that's the whole story."

Maybe. But it is possible to suggest that maybe there was something more than talent. Most of that great Oakland team is still around, but on other clubs. The players were traded away, sold, or released as free agents. How are these very talented players doing away from the A's? A glance at the major-league averages in August 1977 suggested that none were exactly burning up the leagues for their new clubs. Claudell Washington was doing the best, batting .290 with six homers for Texas. Reggie Jackson, made a millionaire by the Yankees, was batting .287 with 17 home runs and 53 runs batted in, although he finished the season strong. Joe Rudi was batting .264 with 13 homers for the California Angels, Bert Campaneris was batting .251 for Texas, Sal Bando was hitting .245 with 12 homers for Milwaukee, and Gene Tenace had 10 homers and a .218 average for San Diego.

Among the pitchers on other clubs, Hunter had a 6–5 record and a 4.66 earned-run average for the Yankees, while Rollie Fingers at San Diego was 7–4 with a 2.98 ERA. There may have been many causes, but the simple fact is that individually and collectively the former A's stars were performing well below their standard of play with Oakland. Could there have been some chemistry at work out on the Bay that made them so much more talented?

Chemistry is the word, for the explosive ingredient on the Oakland club was the owner-general manager, Charles Oscar Finley, surely one of the most controversial individuals ever to own a sports franchise. The Oakland A's *are* Charlie Finley. He made the ball club and he turned around and destroyed it. The club in its championship years reflected his personality. If there was an ingredient other than talent that made the team click, it came from Finley.

He never tires of telling all who will listen that he is a self-made man. He grew up in Birmingham, Alabama, and Gary, Indiana, the grandson of an Irish immigrant steelworker. He worked in the steel mills as a young man. He sold magazines and insurance. He worked so hard at be-

Leading the cheering at the 1974 World Series is—who else? Charles Oscar Finley surrounded by his family, friends, and fans. And he had a lot to cheer about. He owned the team, didn't he? (*Photo by Jonathan Perry*)

coming a success that he succumbed to a severe case of tuberculosis and spent two years in a sanitarium in Indiana. While flat on his back, the hard-driving Finley had the idea that would make his fortune: selling group disability insurance to doctors.

Released from the hospital in 1948, he visited doctor after doctor till he made his first group sale to the Lake County Medical Society in Indiana. By 1951, he was selling his first national plan and making a million dollars a year in commissions. Today, Finley is many times a millionaire and will tell all his "Three S" philosophy of life. "Sweat plus Sacrifice equal Success." A more likely explanation lies in the endless hours Finley worked at selling insurance, the highly individualistic control he kept over all facets of his operation, and the rigid cost accounting he used to avoid wasting a penny.

Inside this splendidly successful insurance salesman lurked a former batboy for the Birmingham Barons of the Southern Association and a former first baseman for the semipro LaPorte, Indiana, Cubs. Considering himself not good enough to be a major-league ballplayer, Finley wanted the next best substitute. He wanted to own a baseball team. Four times he tried, bidding to buy the Philadelphia Athletics, Detroit Tigers, Chicago White Sox, and California Angels. His bids were either too small or they came too late.

There was probably another explanation for Finley's failure to own a club. The other team owners wanted him in baseball about as much as a movie starlet wants a black eye. Finley was an outspoken maverick. He openly scoffed at baseball, which is run by the various owners, as hidebound to tradition, prepared to let the sport lose the interest of the fans rather than change and keep up with the times. Finley gave a one-word description of baseball: dull.

He felt the sport was losing out to football, basketball, and hockey because pitching dominated the game, choking the action out of it. He believed baseball must take steps to increase the hitting and base running and runs scored if it was to match the action of the other major sports.

One of his ideas was adopted by the American League with significant effects. For years, Finley said it was ridiculous for a pitcher to bat, creating an automatic, rally-busting out. Have someone bat for him, so there would be nine hitters in the lineup. Today the American League uses the designated hitter—Finley's idea.

He has no shortage of ideas. He believes it is ridiculous to give a pitcher four balls for a walk while a batter gets only three strikes. He wants three balls for a walk to force the pitchers to put the ball over the plate. It will speed up the game and give hitters more of a chance. He believes the twenty-second clock should be introduced into baseball. Under the rules, a pitcher has twenty seconds to deliver the next pitch. It is not enforced, leaving pitchers to scratch themselves and pick lint off their uniform while fans fall asleep. Finley wants a clock installed on the scoreboard, much like the twenty-four-second clock in professional basketball. If the pitcher doesn't get the ball off in twenty seconds, he is charged with a ball. Finley wants orange baseballs, instead of white. He maintains orange balls will be easier to hit at night. These three ideas haven't been adopted, but don't bet at least some of them won't one day.

After all, who would have bet not very many years ago that players would take the field wearing bright-colored uniforms and white shoes? The Oakland A's did, wearing green-and-yellow uniforms personally designed by Finley. Most teams are now brightly attired.

And night games in the World Series. That was another Finley idea. And fireworks during and after the games and promotions and giveaways to bring in the fans and a gigantic scoreboard that shoots off fireworks and attractive girls to retrieve foul balls and a mule called "Charley O" as a team mascot and offering bonuses to players to grow exotic mustaches. These and many other innovations originated either with Finley or the other resident maverick among baseball owners, Bill Veeck. Veeck launched many promotional schemes (including a midget batter and a one-armed outfielder) while owner of the Cleveland Indians, the St. Louis Browns, and then the Chicago White Sox. Like him or not, Finley has been a fresh breeze, or maybe a tornado, in the staid halls of baseball.

Finley got his chance to buy a club in 1960, the last-place Kansas City A's. It cost him $2 million and the team lost each year more money than Finley made off his insurance business. In 1965, the A's, formerly of Philadelphia, formerly of Kansas City, became the Oakland A's. The team has never drawn well in California. Even in its championship years, the A's never pulled in a million fans a season. Finley is said to be trying to move the club to Washington, D.C., or any of a half-dozen other cities. It really won't matter, for wherever the team happens to reside, it is really the *Finley A's*. Everything about the whole organization is an extension of Charles O. Finley.

A great deal has been written ridiculing Finley the baseball man, and at least as many words have been penned complaining about Finley as a penurious tyrant. But if a person starts with the premise—as indeed Finley does—that it was his hard-earned money that bought the team, giving him the right to run it however he thinks best, then it all becomes comprehensible as well as fascinating. Said another way, Finley is running his team to please, in order, Charles O. Finley and the fans. He is most definitely not running it to please the players or the other baseball moguls.

Finley loves to tell how he listened to all sorts of advice when he entered baseball. He needed a good general manager and a good field manager and lots of people experienced in the exotic niceties of operating a baseball team. Finley followed the advice and discovered (a) it didn't create a very good baseball team and (b) it cost a lot of money. More than that, owning the team wasn't any fun for Finley.

Finley fired Frank Lane, his highly respected general manager, and declared Charles O. Finley the general manager. He put a figurative swinging door on the dugout to accommodate the comings and goings of his field manager, twelve in fifteen seasons, then sportswriters wearied of keeping count of them. Finley made it known that he didn't believe there was any particular magic involved in managing a team. He suggested he could install a traffic cop in front of the dugout to wave relief pitchers into the game and still win the pennant. And about the same level of expertise was required from general managers, broadcasters, farm directors, scouts, ticket managers, publicity directors, and everyone else connected with a baseball club.

All of this was a blow to baseball's solar plexus. It did take the breath away to suggest that traffic cops, taxi drivers, steel-mill workers, and nineteen-year-old college girls, all of whom Finley listened to and hired for his front office, could run a baseball team. The sport had long resembled a gentlemen's club. Some team owners ran their organization as a *pater familias*. Cronies of owners tended to stay on the job long past the normal age of retirement. Room could seemingly always be found in the organization for a retired player. Baseball clubs were never noted as lean and hard, but rather as fat and bloated, loaded with unnecessary personnel employed at high salaries and running up horrendous expenses.

A Finley hater can say he was penurious or even stingy or maybe a tightwad. A more reasoning approach was that he was intelligently thrifty and careful with a dollar. The A's had never drawn well. The team didn't produce the huge sums that seem naturally to occur in New York, Detroit, or Los Angeles. Yet Finley made money every year in Oakland—$600,000 a year is the figure usually given—by cutting expenses. He has the smallest front-office organization in baseball. Every expense, including stationery and perhaps even pencils and paper clips, has to be approved by Finley. Meals for the press (who have a reputation, richly undeserved, to be sure, as freeloaders) were cut back to no more than fifty repasts of cold cuts and chicken. The phone was taken out of the clubhouse, and the team flew regularly scheduled flights whenever possible rather than expensive charters.

The public grousing about all this has been merely monumental. If a person starts with the premise that a multimillionaire sportsman owning a baseball club ought to lavish his money on the luxuries that go with high living, then Charlie Finley is a mean man. However, if a person starts with the premise that an owner ought to field a good team, win pennants, and show a profit while doing it, then Finley is a wizard.

Finley's reputation for—well—thrift has made the most headlines in his prolonged and regular salary disputes with his players. Fracases over wages are as old as baseball. Finley has merely reduced (or elevated?) them to a science or maybe an art. The player feels—and who is to argue with it?—that he deals in a precious commodity, a very few years when his skills are at their peak. Arms and legs lose their strength, and reflexes slow. The player, once a star, is past his prime in his midthirties and out of the majors (with few exceptions) before he is forty. Considering the

They played to win, those Oakland A's did. Reggie Jackson, sliding safely into home plate in the 1974 World Series against the Dodgers, and a catapulting Sal Bando show just how much. (*Photo by Jonathan Perry*)

years it took him to hone his skills, the player usually has no more than a dozen, seldom only five really prime years. The player feels that to be a major-league baseball star requires special skills. Few people have the talent. He wants payment for the uniqueness and preciousness of his skills. With the expansion of major-league baseball and the reduction in the number of minor-league teams, baseball talent has become greatly diluted at a time when baseball owners are receiving big money from television rights. Players want their share. Result: Salaries of $100,000 for journeyman players and as much as $500,000 a season for superstars playing under multimillion-dollar, multi-year contracts.

Simultaneous with this escalation in wages—and, indeed, a cause of it—is the dilution of the historic reserve clause in baseball contracts. Until a few years ago, baseball clubs owned the players. Under the reserve clause, the player could sell his services to no other team. He could refuse to play and retire, but he was stuck with the team that owned him. At the same time, the owner could sell or trade the player at will. There were advantages to this system. Teams had a continuity of personnel. But players increasingly came to feel that theirs was a form of human slavery. They should be able to quit their job and shop around for a better one just like a cab driver, an accountant, or a lawyer. In time, the courts came to agree with them. Now players can play out their option, after which they are free to sign with whatever club they want, including their old club.

Charlie Finley had a lot to do with all this. His ideas on player remuneration failed to coincide with those of most of his players. For starters, he felt that the big bonuses paid to players upon signing with the team—$85,000 to Reggie Jackson, for example—was something like an advance on future salaries, not an outright gift for scrawling their signature on a contract. Worse, he felt the players were employees, and when he paid them $50,000 or $100,000 to play 162 games, he was entitled to a certain level of performance. A good day at bat, even a good season, was not an automatic qualification for a fatter pay envelope.

Too, Finley liked to point to the fringe benefits. Players had a lot of creature comforts provided at the owner's expense. They had their medical expenses paid if hurt, and their salary continued even if they were lost for the whole season. Then there was the little matter of the rule forbidding a player's salary to be cut more than 20 per cent in a year. If a good year led to a 50 per cent raise, then a bad year could result only in a 20 per cent cut. To Finley, this was unfair to owners.

His battles with his players were minor legends. Jackson held out in 1970, Vida Blue in 1972. Both gave in for less than they demanded, but they were bitter toward Finley, for they felt he had humiliated them publicly by ridiculing their ability and their salary demands. When baseball adopted binding arbitration to settle contract disputes in 1974, the A's players became the biggest users of the procedure. In that first year, arbitration raised Jackson's salary from $75,000 to $135,000, Bando's from $60,000 to $100,000, and Holtzman's from $66,500 to $93,000. The next year Bando and Holtzman returned to the arbitrators, but were given no raises. Finley was delighted. "Sure, Bando had some clutch hits," he said. "Don't I deserve something for $100,000?" The Holtzman decision was positive vindication for him, Finley felt. Holtzman had won twenty-one games in 1973 and got his raise the next year. When he then won nineteen games, Finley failed to see how a raise was in order. As he has put it, "I don't see I'm a charitable organization." He says he has loaned money to players, given them tips on the stock market, and helped with their business affairs. Don't such acts count for something in salary disputes?

Finley was fighting a losing battle. The first to go was Catfish Hunter, perhaps the premier pitcher in the American League. He discovered Finley had committed a breach in his contract and had it abrogated. He then sold himself to the New York Yankees for $3 million or so. By 1976, the dam broke for Finley. No less than seven of his premier stars were playing out their options. At the end of the season, they would be worth precisely zero to him. Hours before the June 15 trading deadline, he peddled Joe Rudi and Rollie Fingers to the Boston Red Sox for $1 million each and Vida Blue to the Yankees for $1.5 million. Since the Yankees already had Hunter and had picked up Ken Holtzman in a trade with the Orioles, the A's championship pitching staff was suddenly the starting rotation for the Yankees.

Everyone howled, most of all Bowie Kuhn, the baseball commissioner hired by the owners. He reversed the sale and ordered the players to remain with Oakland. The Finley-Kuhn rhubarb was a tasty one. Kuhn said he was acting in the best interests of baseball. The pennant was being handed to either Boston or New York, while Oakland was reduced to rubble. Other teams had no chance. Baseball was losing whatever aura of sportsmanship it had left. It wasn't a game but a cut-throat business.

On the other hand, Finley was being done out of $3.5 million and left to receive nothing for his investment in his players. Owners had always been able to sell and trade players, making the best deal they could. Selling and trading the game's superstars was a fixture in baseball. The Red Sox sent Babe Ruth to the Yankees, who ultimately dispatched him to the Boston Braves. Connie Mack, former A's owner, had traded his stars away, including Jimmy

Foxx, Joe Cronin, and Lefty Grove to the Red Sox. Yet Finley was denied the right to do the same. Worse, the A's were left in a truly desperate condition. The seven stars were going to leave and, except for Blue, did leave. Finley said he intended to use the $3.5 million to develop new, young players. He could hardly do that when Kuhn left him with nothing. Ultimately, Blue was traded in 1978.

In the year or so since the celebrated nonsale of the players, Finley's image has improved. He has hardly become a folk hero among baseball fans, but he is being spoken of more sympathetically. The tremendous escalation of salaries since the option clause went into effect has left fans in something approaching a turmoil. Common complaints are that the salaries are out of hand, that nobody, but nobody is worth $500,000 a year for doing anything, including playing baseball. After all, the President of the United States only gets $200,000. The former free agents, in the main, are not setting their leagues on fire. Some of them are getting soundly booed by the fans. One feels positively sorry for Wayne Garland, a $1 million pitcher Cleveland grabbed from the Orioles. He could hardly win for losing in 1977, and the Cleveland fans let him have it. He came up sore-armed in 1978 and was lost for the season.

Most telling, few of the teams who invested most heavily in free agents seem likely to win the pennant. Cleveland, for example, is mired in the second division, while the Orioles, expected to be crippled by the loss of Garland and two other stars, has fielded a young team that fought all season for the division lead. To sum up, if a fan starts with the premise that high salaries and open bidding for free agents are not good for baseball, then the conclusion that maybe Charlie Finley knew something is not hard to reach.

It was not just Finley's penny pinching that made him something less than a font of popularity throughout the

Oakland organization. He had a talent for harassment. Finley is an absentee owner and general manager. His business is based in Chicago, and he owns a home in LaPorte, Indiana. Probably one of the bigger sorrows of his life is his failure, thus far, to acquire either of the Chicago teams. Being able to visit Oakland only irregularly, he phones. Does he ever! Charlie is not thrifty about the telephone. He calls anyone connected with the team at any hour of the day or night.

That includes his field managers. A widely believed piece of sports wisdom is that owners and general managers should not mess with the day-to-day operations on the field. The game itself should be left to coaches and managers. Only disaster can result from front-office interference. Charlie Finley does not believe that bit of conventional wisdom. He calls his managers with instructions on whom to play and when. The lineup is of acute interest to him, and he has been known to call up for pinch-hitters and pinch-runners. And if a manager's piece of strategy does not work, his explanations to Finley had better be good.

Finley exercises his prerogative to stick his finger into every facet of the Oakland A's, especially if it involves a financial outlay, and he is mostly dissatisfied with the activities of anyone who works for him. By all reports, hiring on with Finley is hardly the ticket to a relaxed life of easy contemplation. He drives his people wild and most quit in disgust, their nerves shot in the bloom of youth.

Worse than his nit-picking interference, his insistence on making even minor decisions himself, is his manner with people. The testimony is impeccable. Charlie Finley was a devoted husband, at least until his divorce after thirty years of marriage, and a doting father to his seven children. He enjoys a drink and the conviviality that goes with it and can be a "good-time Charlie" when the occasion demands it. Cab drivers race to have him for a fare, for he is a big tipper. More, he'll probably call the dugout and activate the cabbie's suggestions for the lineup that evening. Finley can be compulsively generous, as well as kind, thoughtful, and compassionate. Even dogs love him.

Charlie Finley can also be rough, brutal, cruel, brusk, and obscene with those who work for him. His "chewing out" can leave an employee—and baseball players are employees—humiliated and barren of self-respect. Vida Blue's hatred for Finley is well known. It was not just that Finley humiliated him in contract disputes, but also that he did it in such a way as to leave Blue feeling like a "nigger" enslaved on the plantation. Dislike, disgust, even hatred for Finley were rampant on the Oakland team during its best years. Mention his name in the dugout and the response would be "screw that bastard" or worse.

Oh the squabbling. In the second game of the 1973 World Series against the Mets, Mike Andrews made two errors at second. That evening, Finley prevailed upon the team physician to declare Andrews unfit to play because of a sore arm. Finley dropped him from the team and brought up another, hopefully error-free second baseman. In protest the A's wore No. 17, Andrews' number, on their sleeves at the next day's workout. Andrews was ordered reinstated to the team. Finley looked bad, and his players had shown the world how transparent his ruse was. He retaliated later. In 1972, he had given each player a championship ring set with a diamond worth $3,000. In 1973 and 1974 they got a ring *sans* diamond.

But enough. Whole books have been written purveying the eccentricities of Charlie Finley. If a person wants to find evidence that he is a cataclysmic personality who thrives on turmoil and that he runs a bad baseball organization and infuriates his players, then that person has undertaken a simple task. Yet Finley put together one of the great teams of the recent era. Of any era. The number of teams that have won three world championships in a row can be counted on precisely three fingers. The Yankees won four in a row, 1936–39, and five in a row, 1949–53. Since the A's are an expression of Finley, he must have done something right. What?

For starters, Finley has to be acknowledged as a peerless judge of young baseball talent and indefatigable in signing it. That team wasn't put together by magic. Charles O. Finley and no one else gets the credit. In 1962, he heard about a catcher for a team in Cuba. He signed him for $500, flew him to the United States, and converted him into Bert Campaneris, one of the game's premier shortstops and base stealers. Two years later, he signed Jim Hunter just out of high school. Scouts had given up on Hunter after he accidentally shot himself in the foot. Finley gave him $75,000 for signing, told him to call himself "Catfish," and sent him to the Mayo Clinic to have his foot mended. The next year, Finley signed Gene Tenace, Joe Rudi (other scouts ignored him after he broke his hand), and Rollie Fingers. All were just out of high school, and their combined bonuses came to a bargain-basement $37,000.

When the baseball draft began in 1965, Finley signed Rick Monday (later traded for Holtzman) and Sal Bando. The next year he picked up Jackson for $85,000. Claudell Washington was obtained for an inconceivable $3,000, Vida Blue for $37,000, and Blue Moon Odom for $75,000.

Finley was also a wheeler-dealer. Players were employees, or maybe property, and Finley seldom let sentiment interfere with winning. He'd make any trade that he figured would help the club. He liked good young players who worked cheap and also older players who had a season or two left in them. No team was ever set, Finley maintained.

Of the twenty-six players who won the World Series in 1972, only nine remained on the 1975 team. By 1977 there were only three; Blue, Bill North, and Angel Mangual. But then some of his former players may be back. Finley has a history. He fired and rehired two managers, Hank Bauer and Alvin Dark. He sold Tommy Davis and his $72,000 contract to the Cubs. When the Cubs released him, Finley rehired him for $37,500.

For all his trading, the nucleus of the A's consisted of those players Finley signed as teen-agers. That is in the baseball tradition. Conventional wisdom has it that a winner can't be bought. It has to be developed on the farm. See, not all conventional wisdom was lost on Finley.

Dal Maxvill on why the A's were winners: "Charlie is a good judge of talent. He signed the nucleus of that team out of high school and college. They played together in the minors and at Kansas City, where the team was dead last. They weren't very good. Then all of a sudden they all matured together and they were winners. Along the way some frictions developed. They had played together so long a number of them got so they couldn't stand each other. But that was off the field or in the locker room. On the field they played baseball."

Catfish Hunter: "We had a way of getting it out of our system. There'd be an argument and then a fight, but after that it was all baseball. We all wanted to win. That was the name of the game. And the way to win was to give baseball 100 per cent and pull together. A player had better not carry his grudge out on the field and fail to give his 100 per cent or he'd hear it from the rest of us."

That quarreling, fighting bunch of talented players wanted to win. They wanted to hit Charlie Finley up for a raise and they wanted the glory of being world champions. They won. Did they ever! The Oakland A's sound more

The epitome of team spirit. The Oakland A's win their third World Series game in 1974. Left to right are Glenn Abbott, Wes Stock, Rollie Fingers, Ken Holtzman, Catfish Hunter, Larry Haney, two batboys, Joe Rudi, and Dick Green. Where are they all today? (*Photo by Jonathan Perry*)

than a little familiar. Gene Woodling spoke of the Yankees of twenty years earlier as a "bunch of RA's"—fighting-mad red asses. They won because they were too fighting mad to be beat. Oakland was another collection of RA's.

Recall that older Yankee era in another way. The burr under the Yankee saddle was Casey Stengel. The "Ol' Perfesser" had a talent for enraging the likes of Woodling, Bauer, Mantle, Rizzuto, Richardson, Reynolds, and Raschi into five consecutive world championships. Casey Stengel and Charlie Finley may be radically different human beings, but perhaps they engaged in the same process. With his penuriousness, his petty interferences, his various cruelties in human relationships, his egomania about hogging the spotlight, Finley earned the dislike of his players. He made them mad. And the madder they got, the more they won. This is all just a theory, but could it be that there was method to the madness of Charles O. Finley?

By way of answer, consider the fact that the Oakland A's, still very much run by Finley in his inimitable manner, were in the thick of the race in the American League West. His former stars may be long gone, but Finley has recruited another powerhouse of rookies, has-beens, and little-knowns.

WHAT MAKES A TEAM?

What is to be concluded from all these quotes from outstanding players, thoughts of coaches, and team experiences? What makes a team? What is teamwork?

The experiences of each of these teams were different. There is obviously not one way to make a team but several ways. A common ingredient in all these teams is the talent of the players. Individual talent without teamwork will not win. We have seen that time and again. But the players must be good. A group of overweight, slow-footed, and awkward people are not going to win very often, no matter how much they may desire to win and how much teamwork they may possess.

Organization is clearly vital to teamwork. The people behind the scenes, the club presidents and general managers, the clubhouse personnel, the equipment managers, and the ticket sellers all must do their job or the team is not going to be successful. They must pull together as much as the players. If these front-office people are divided, if they are only out for themselves, then the team is going to reflect these attitudes.

A story illustrates this. One of the successful sports franchises in history has been the Los Angeles Rams of the National Football League. But it was not always so. Dan Reeves, heir to a chain of supermarkets, bought the team as the Cleveland Rams in 1940. It did little but lose money, $40,000 the first year. By 1945, when the Rams won the NFL championship, the losses had grown to $64,000. Reeves, heir to a chain of supermarkets, bought the team as losses grew to $128,000.

The red ink continued to flow, and Reeves faced a fiscal crisis. The federal government believes a businessman is foolish to continue to own a money-losing business. If he loses $50,000 a year for five years, the government says he has a hobby, not a business, and collects income taxes on all the money he has lost for those five years. Faced with a huge tax payment, Reeves took in partners until his personal loss in the fifth year was under $50,000. His partners did not invest money in the Rams. They merely assumed a share of the losses in hopes of a future share of the profits.

The Los Angeles Rams lost money through 1949, then turned the corner. Beginning in 1950, the Rams became highly profitable. The partners who had assumed a share of the losses were now making a great deal of money. By 1957, the Rams were drawing more than a million fans to eighteen regular-season and exhibition games. The partners who had assumed losses totaling $353,000 received profits of over $2 million in the next twelve years. During this time the Rams were an extremely successful football team, winning the championship or challenging for it year after year.

What can only be described as jealousy set in. Reeves' share of the club may have shrunk from 100 to 30 per cent, but he was still the general manager. He ran it to suit himself, and he received a lot of publicity. The team was Dan Reeves' Rams. His partners objected to his celebrity status. They got together and voted Reeves out as general manager in 1955. Reeves spent the next seven years raising the capital to buy back his team, and he did so in 1962.

What is interesting is the decline of the Rams football team during the years of turmoil among the principal owners. In 1955, the Rams won the conference title with an 8–3–1 record. The next year they were 6–6. They did well in 1958 with an 8–4 record, but in 1959 they fell to the cellar with a disastrous 2–10 season. The team was 4–7–1 in 1960, 4–10 in 1961, and an unbelievable 1–12–1 in 1962. Attendance dropped from 1,061,000 in 1959 to 820,000 in 1962.

Reasons for the decline were not hard to find. No one was at the helm of the team. Disastrous trades were made. Scouting for the draft tailed off sharply. The team itself divided into cliques. Players or groups of them called one of the owners who favored them. Dissension ruled the club. Coaches came to resemble referees of the various squabbles. When Reeves regained control of the club, the team's fortune improved radically. The Rams have been an NFL power ever since under Reeves and former Colt owner Carroll Rosenbloom, who took over upon Reeves' death.

The Los Angeles experience is hardly the only one. The decline of the Yankees after 1964 has been much analyzed. Many observers believe a root cause was the sale of the team to CBS. When George Steinbrenner bought control and took a personal interest in the team, the Yankee fortunes improved.

The success story of the Dallas Cowboys lies in the team's continuity of ownership, management, and coaching. The Montreal Canadiens speak of their organization as a big happy family. The Boston Celtics have been dynastic, in part because Red Auerbach has been general manager all those years, as well as coach for many of them. The Colts speak of the importance of Carroll Rosenbloom to their great years. The personal interest and involvement of Bill Simpson have been vital to the dynastic success of the Raybestos Brakettes. Woody Hayes at Ohio State dedicated his autobiography to Dick Larkin, his longtime boss and athletic director at the university. Charlie Finley made his Oakland A's his personal fiefdom and created a successful team. Clearly, a successful team lies in an important way in the people who run it.

The coaches and players interviewed for this book have spoken repeatedly of the importance of the selection of personnel. To be sure, every coach or manager would jump at a chance to possess those rare superstars: a Babe Ruth, a Johnny Unitas, a Jim Brown, a Wilt Chamberlain, a Kareem Abdul-Jabbar, a Maurice Richard. Such individuals are hard to find, and their presence on a team does not guarantee a dynasty. Consider such giants as Bob Feller, Ted Williams, Stan Musial, Hank Aaron, Willie Mays, Elgin Baylor, Jerry West, Gale Sayers, Bobby Hull, Gordie Howe, and two score other superstars who failed to make their teams more than occasional champions.

Something more than ability is needed. The Yankees looked for a certain character, poor boys who were gentlemen and had a thirst to win. No hotfoots and boyish pranks were allowed. At UCLA, John Wooden wanted quickness ahead of speed or size in his basketball players, but even more, he wanted a certain unselfishness that permitted the player to surrender his ego to achieve teamwork. Woody Hayes wants the "quality kid" who comes from a closely knit family and who values a college education. Ralph Raymond also wants his Brakettes to come from closely knit families, as well as to have heart and guts and pride and willingness to work hard. Tom Landry wants the sort of character that rises above adversity. The Canadiens recruited Quebec boys who lived at home and were sensitive to the desires of Quebec fans for a winner. Colt players were friends, their nucleus bound by religious zeal as much as a desire to win. The Celtics wanted men, perhaps of less talent, who understood the philosophy that winning meant giving 100 per cent of yourself all the time, keeping nothing in reserve.

Despite the different interpretations of the meaning of character, each of these dynastic teams selected personnel who fit the mold. The nucleus of the team were personal friends. The element of a big happy family was important to many teams. Players shared common interest and goals. They frequently lived near each other. As Bill Russell said, "Above all, we are friends." Pete Rose speaks of the same quality among the current Cincinnati Reds. Friction, jealousies, and dissension are minimized among the great teams, except the Oakland A's. The good teams consciously select the personnel to achieve this unity.

Leadership is another key ingredient. Many, although not all the dynastic teams had a player or players who was the team leader on the field, court, rink, or diamond. He was the example for the others, their inspiration. He perhaps had natural leadership abilities and came quickly to his position of trust. One thinks of John Unitas or Maurice Richard in this way. For others, the respect—and how many times the word *love* was used in speaking of a leader—came from a history of coming through in the clutch, of demanding more of themselves, of carrying the load for the team, of exemplifying the best the team stood for.

Consider the regard, respect, and love granted by their teammates to Lou Gehrig, Joe DiMaggio, Mickey Mantle,

John Unitas, Bertha Tickey, Joan Joyce, Maurice Richard, Bill Russell, John Havlicek, and Bill Walton. They earned it in game after game. They asked more of themselves than of others. They produced when others failed. Few men in any line of endeavor ever earn the respect of their peers that these outstanding individuals did. And every one of them was a team player. Their personal success was sour in their mouths if the team didn't win.

Again and again we heard of the desire to win. It would seem to be as common in athletics as dirt or grass or ice. After all, doesn't anyone want to win? Who enters a game to lose? Yet there seems to be something else at work on the dynastic teams. Gene Woodling said the Yankees of the 1950s were a bunch of RA's, red asses, so mad they couldn't be beaten. When the going got tough, they got tougher. The Oakland A's had this quality. They fought like alley cats off—but also on—the field. And in both these instances, the players policed each other's efforts. If a player didn't put out, didn't get mad at losing and try his hardest, he heard it from his teammates. Remember Joe DiMaggio chewing out a young Yogi Berra for being too weary to catch a doubleheader? For the Boston Celtics, according to Bob Cousy, the term is "killer instinct," a willingness to do absolutely anything to win.

Apparently there are dimensions to the desire to win. There is wanting to win, then there is, for want of a better term, the killer instinct. Among the dynasties, there is apparently an ability among whole teams of players to psych themselves up to a controlled rage, a superhuman effort that wins a big game. One thinks of Jerry Kramer's block that opened up a hole for Bart Starr and one more Green Bay championship. Or there is old Sam Jones' off-balance shot that lucked into the basket to further another Celtic championship. Or Maurice Richard, embarrassed for his team, scoring five goals in a playoff game to personally lead his team to a championship. And it isn't just an individual, it's a team. Consider the frustrated Colts of 1970 getting it up for a whole season to be Super Bowl champs. Or the tears in the Brakettes' dugout because someone made an error that let the team down. Or Dallas, coming off the floor following a humiliating defeat on "Monday Night Football" to prove they could win the big ones. More than desire to win, both these football teams desired not to be labeled as losers. Or those incredible Celtics, old by any standard, tired beyond caring, all bandages and aches, getting it together one last time for a championship. *Cosa nostra* indeed.

What is it that makes such feats possible? Adrenalin, to be sure. But how do such players, such teams of players get it flowing in a controlled, winning fashion? Words fail: desire, pride, tradition, will, teamwork, killer instinct, *cosa nostra,* character. By whatever name, the dynastic teams have it.

Coaches. The great teams have great coaches. Joe McCarthy and Casey Stengel, Red Auerbach and Bill Russell, Woody Hayes, John Wooden, Dick Irvin and Toe Blake, Weeb Ewbank and Don Shula, Ralph Raymond, Tom Landry. Of course, the A's weren't particularly associated with great managers, but then they had Charlie Finley.

What did these great coaches have in common? They all knew their respective games. But lots of coaches do that. They knew how to select personnel who would fit together under their guidance. They knew the misfit, however talented he might be, and got rid of him. There was no room for bad apples in their barrels. Most of all, they knew how to motivate the players they had selected. Some do it loudly, like a Woody Hayes or a Vince Lombardi. Others are quiet, *à la* John Wooden or Tom Landry. Some impress their players with their memories, like Joe McCarthy and Casey Stengel. Others impress them with their expertise, like Shula and Landry.

Woody Hayes makes it very simple so anyone can learn it with repetition. Landry makes it complex so they can't learn it easily. Stengel was a master psychologist. Lombardi had one idea: win. Raymond does it by setting a high standard and expecting his girls to achieve it. He demands a lot. As we have seen, Landry and Wooden, both quiet men, intimidated their players with criticism of their mistakes. Hayes does it with a blow to the belly. But all are intimidating. Fear seems to be important, fear of the coach, fear of criticism, fear of losing, fear of not being a Yankee. Auerbach was authoritarian. He told his Celtics what to do. He was not running a democracy.

There seems to be no one secret to motivation. Each coach does it differently as suits his personality and the players he has selected. He uses whatever he can: fear, encouragement, a fatherly pat on the back, public criticism, ridicule, rah-rah school spirit. Some of these coaches are conservative, others flamboyant, but in their own ways they are knowledgeable, authoritarian men with strong personalities.

If it weren't for the Oakland A's, I'd end the book right here. But that incredible team broke the above rules and still won. There must be something else to a successful team. Indeed, there is. There are perhaps other and better terms to describe it, but the prime ingredient in each of these dynastic teams was a unifying force. In each case something was introduced that unified these raw individuals into a team. They all wanted to win, to be sure. Again, who doesn't? But each of these super, dynastic teams had something else that unified them.

On the Yankees it was pride and tradition and, face it, the desire to be a Yankee and fear of not being one. On the Celtics the unifying force was their cosa nostra, their philosophy of demanding more of themselves than their opponents would give of themselves. On the Colts it was their regard and love for two remarkable individuals, Carroll Rosenbloom and John Unitas. In Montreal, the unifying force was the expectation of the fans and the people of the province of Quebec.

At Ohio State, the unifying force is the person of Woody Hayes, his temper tantrums, his hatred of the school "up North," his demand for quality in athletics and all of education. More important, I do believe, is his intimidation by physical fear and his incessant practice of a few basic plays till they are automatic. The team is unified by fear and boredom.

At UCLA it was a tradition of excellence—first in the land—John Wooden's insistence on unselfish team play. On the Brakettes, it is pride, their commitment, and their will to win that harrowing array of 1–0 ball games. In Dallas, the Cowboys are unified by the complexity of Landry's offense and defense. It is so hard to learn. All are in the same boat. All must pull together to learn it. Also, Dallas was unified by a desire to shed its reputation as a loser.

Oakland. Yes, Oakland. They were unified by their common annoyance, dislike, disgust, and even hatred for Charlie Finley. In his own way he made them just as much a bunch of RA's as Casey Stengel did by his platooning and substituting and pinch-hitting in the first inning.

In one way or another, the dynastic teams achieve a unifying force that cements them as a team, makes them play together, and causes them to try harder. The cement begins with the selection of players. It is enhanced by coaching,

the expectation of fans, the support of the front-office organization, the team's own history of winning and overcom-
ing adversity. The great teams all have it.

Clearly, teamwork doesn't just happen. It is created
through organization, an atmosphere of common purpose,
and a generous application of some form of unifying cement.

To me, the search for teamwork has been inspirational.
We live in an increasingly collective society. Badly, we need
to work together. The team-making methods used by the
splendid organizations in this book have an application far
removed from the playing fields of the United States.

READINGS

Bengtson, Phil, with Hunt, Todd. *Packer Dynasty*. Garden City, N.Y.: Doubleday & Company, 1969.

Brondfield, Jerry. *Woody Hayes and the 100-Yard War*. New York: Random House, 1974.

Chapin, Dwight, and Prugh, Jeff. *The Wizard of Westwood*. Boston, Mass.: Houghton Mifflin Company, 1973.

Golenbock, Peter. *Dynasty: The New York Yankees, 1949–64*. Englewood Cliffs, N.J.: Prentice-Hall, 1975.

Graham, Frank. *The New York Yankees: An Informal History*. New York: G. P. Putnam's Sons, 1958.

Harris, Merv (ed.). *On Court with the Superstars of the NBA*. New York: Viking Press, 1973.

Hayes, Woody. *You Win with People!* Self-publication, 1973.

Levy, Bill. *Three Yards and a Cloud of Dust*. Cleveland, O. World Publishing Company, 1966.

Libby, Bill. *Charlie O. and the Angry A's*. Garden City, N.Y.: Doubleday & Company, 1975.

Liston, Robert A. *The Pros*. New York: Platt & Munk, 1968.

Meany, Tom. *The Yankee Story*. New York: E. P. Dutton & Co., 1960.

Meyers, Jeff. *Dallas Cowboys*. New York: Macmillan Publishing Co., 1974.

Perkins, Steve. *Next Year's Champions: The Story of the Dallas Cowboys*. Cleveland, O.: World Publishing Company, 1969.

Rizzuto, Phil, and Silverman, Al. *The "Miracle" New York Yankees*. New York: Coward-McCann, 1962.

Vare, Robert. *Buckeye*. New York: Harper's Magazine Press, 1974.

Weigel, J. Timothy. *The Buckeyes*. Chicago, Ill.: Henry Regnery Co., 1974.

ROBERT A. LISTON was born in Youngstown, Ohio, in 1927. A graduate of Hiram College, he was a newspaperman from 1954 to 1964, mostly with the Baltimore *News American*. Mr. Liston began selling to leading magazines in 1957 and turned full-time free-lance in 1964. He has written something over forty books, but in truth has lost count. One of his main reasons for writing is independence.

Mr. Liston has lived in some rather exotic places, traveled a lot, and enjoyed himself while writing. Aside from just living abroad in elegant villas, he has also camped with his wife and daughter throughout the United Kingdom, Norway, and about as far north as you can go by car in the world. Mr. Liston now enjoys the peaceful life of Shelby, a small town of ten thousand near his origins in Ohio. He is an avid gardener and is currently teaching writing courses at the Mansfield branch of Ohio State University.

INDEX

Aaron, Hank, 10, 34, 228
Abbott, Glenn, 223
Alcindor, Lew. *See* Jabbar, Kareem Abdul-
Allen, Johnny, 13
Allen, Lucius, 97, 98, 99
Allen, Mel, 35
All-Stars. *See* Raybestos Brakettes
Alston, Walter, 196
Ameche, Alan, 64
American Football League, 169
American League, 6, 9, 11, 203, 206, 210, 217, 224
American Softball Association, 182
Andrews, Mike, 220
Arizona State, 90, 93
Ashland Sabres, 201
Atlanta, 171
Auerbach, Arnold "Red," 42–47, 49–54, 57, 61, 228, 231, 232
Autry, Gene, 3

Backstrom, Ralph, 139
Baltimore Colts, 5, 62–86, 123, 156, 169, 171–73, 227–29, 231
Baltimore Orioles, 30, 31, 217, 218
Bando, Sal, 207, 214, 217, 221
Barrow, Ed, 13, 22, 24
Bauer, Hank, 28, 222, 224
Baylor, Elgin, 55, 61, 228
Bearden, Gene, 31–33
Beaty, Zelmo, 49
Beliveau, Jean, 137, 144, 145, 148–50
Bench, Johnny, 164

Berra, Yogi, 18, 28, 33, 35, 36, 39, 166, 230
Berry, Raymond, 64, 78, 79, 162, 163
Bibby, Henry, 100, 102, 111
Birmingham Barons, 209
Blake, Toe, 137, 138, 141, 148–53, 231
Blue, Vida, 216, 217, 218, 220, 221, 222
Boston Braves, 10, 217
Boston Bruins, 141, 142–43
Boston Celtics, 4, 5, 40–61, 87, 104, 111, 129, 181, 182, 228–33
Boston Red Sox, 3, 28, 31, 217
Bouchard, Emile, 137
Bouchard, Pierre, 153
Bouton, Jim, 35
Bowman, Scotty, 150
Boyd, Bob, 101–4
Boyer, Clete, 28
Brandt, Gil, 158, 163
Bridgeport Co-eds, 199
Brimsek, Frank, 141
Brocklin, Norm van, 75
Broncos, 166
Brooklyn Dodgers, 34, 36
Brown, Jim, 228
Brown, Paul, 75–76, 109, 128–29
Bruce, Earle, 118
Brummel, Lisa, 201
Bryant, Em, 59
Bryant, Paul "Bear," 114
Buffalo Bills, 7
Burleson, Tom, 106

California Angels, 3, 207, 209
Campaneris, Bert, 164, 207, 221
Campbell, Clarence, 143, 145
Carey, Andy, 28
Chamberlain, Wilt, 55, 56, 57, 58, 59, 60, 104, 228
Chandler, Don, 67
Chapin, Dwight, 96
Chappell, Len, 49
Chicago Bears, 62, 162
Chicago Black Hawks, 139
Chicago Cubs, 222
Chicago White Sox, 28, 209, 211
Chiefs, 166, 173
Cincinnati Bengals, 71, 128
Cincinnati Reds, 203, 229
Cincinnati Royals, 54–55
Clemson University, 113
Cleveland Browns, 63, 65, 75–76, 79, 128, 169, 171, 173
Cleveland Indians, 10, 11, 13, 26, 28, 30, 31, 211, 218
Cleveland Rams, 226
Coleman, Jerry, 28
Collins, Joe, 28
Cournoyer, Yvan, 153
Cousy, Bob, 41, 42, 43, 46, 47, 48, 53, 230
Cowens, Dave, 52–53
Cozza, Carm, 118
Cronin, Joe, 218
Crosetti, Frank, 11
Cuozzo, Gary, 65
Curtis, Tommy, 100

Dallas Cowboys, 4, 5, 71, 154–80, 227, 231, 233
Dallman, Howie, 104
Dark, Alvin, 222
Davies, Bill, 121
Davis, Tommy, 222
DeBusschere, Dave, 49
Detroit Red Wings, 139, 141, 143
Detroit Tigers, 17, 209
Dickey, Bill, 10–18, 24, 35
Dietzel, Paul, 118

DiMaggio, Joe, 11, 18, 21, 28, 29, 35, 229, 230
Ditka, Mike, 162
Dodgers, 22, 196
Dorsett, Tony, 178, 179, 180
Drollinger, Ralph, 106
Durnan, Bill, 137

Elizabeth City Teachers College, 164
Ellis, Leroy, 49
Enquist, Sue, 194, 202
Erickson, Keith, 60, 90
Ewbank, Weeb, 69, 76, 78, 80, 231
Ezinicki, "Wild Bill," 139

Farmer, Larry (Moose), 89, 100, 102, 109–10, 111
Feller, Bob, 10–12, 228
Fingers, Rollie, 205–7, 217, 221, 223
Finley, Charles Oscar, 37, 207–12, 213, 215–22, 224, 228, 231, 233
Florida A&M, 118
Ford, Whitey, 28
Fort Valley State, 164
49ers, 173
Foxx, Jimmy, 217–18
Fritsch, Toni, 164

Gaechter, Mike, 164
Gagnon, Johnny, 137
Gainey, Bob, 153
Garcia, Mike, 11
Garland, Wayne, 218
Gator Bowl, 113
Gehrig, Lou, 11, 12, 16, 17–18, 20, 35, 229
Gent, Pete, 164
Geoffrion, Bernie "Boom Boom," 137
Golenbock, Peter, 18
Gomez, Lefty, 11
Goodrich, Gail, 55, 90, 91, 92
Goyette, Phil, 139
Graham, Otto, 76

Grambling, 113
Green, Cornell, 164
Green, Dick, 223
Green Bay Packers, 4, 62–63,
    65–67, 69, 121, 156, 166, 168,
    169–71, 174, 196, 230
Greer, Hal, 55
Grove, Lefty, 218

Hagen, Cliff, 50
Hainsworth, George, 137
Haney, Larry, 223
Harlem Globetrotters, 49, 50
Harris, Bucky, 24–26
Harris, Cliff, 164, 176, 177,
    179–80
Hartman, Mary, 188
Harvey, Doug, 139
Havlicek, John, 49, 51, 55, 59, 61,
    230
Hayes, Bob, 164
Hayes, Elvin, 98
Hayes, Woodrow Wilson, 114–20,
    121–23, 167, 228, 231–33
Hazzard, Walt, 90, 91, 108
Heinsohn Tommy, 41–42, 44–45,
    47, 49, 52–53, 104
Heitz, Kenny, 98, 99
Henderson, Murray, 141
Henrich, Tommy "Old Reliable,"
    11, 24
Hebert, Donna, 191
Hess, Bill, 118
Hicke, Bill, 139
Hightower, Wayne, 49
Hill, Calvin, 164
Hirsch, Jack, 90
Hoad, Lew, 164
Hodges, Gil, 36
Hogue, Paul, 49
Hollyfield, Larry, 100
Holtz, Lou, 118
Holtzman, Ken, 205, 216, 217,
    221, 223
Holy Cross, 47
Houk, Ralph, 26–28

Houle, Rejean, 153
Houston, University of, 98
Howard, Elston, 34, 39
Howe, Gordie, 139, 228
Hubbard, Rudy, 118
Hull, Bobby, 139, 228
Hunter, Jim "Catfish," 36–39,
    205–6, 207, 217, 221, 222, 223
Hutton, Maru, 200

Indiana State University, 107
Iowa State University, 118
Irsay, Robert, 79
Irvin, Dick, 137, 142, 150, 153,
    231

Jabbar, Kareem Abdul-, 96–99,
    100, 104, 106, 108, 111, 112,
    228
Jackson, Reggie, 15, 36, 38, 207,
    214–16, 221
Jarvis, Doug, 147
Johnson, Marquis, 106
Johnson, Tom, 139
Johnson C. Smith College, 164
Joliat, Aurel, 137
Jones, Bert, 81–86, 173
Jones, Dub, 81
Jones, K. C., 47, 49, 55, 56
Jones, Sam, 47, 55, 58, 59, 230
Joyce, Joan, 185, 187–93, 199, 230

Kansas City A's, 211
Keane, Johnny, 35
Keller, Charles "King Kong," 11
Keller, H., 15
Kern, Rex, 122, 123, 129, 130,
    131–32
King, Billie Jean, 199
Kramer, Jerry, 171, 230
Kubeck, Tony, 28
Kuhn, Bowie, 217, 218

Lacey, Edgar, 99
Lach, Elmer, 137, 141
Lafleur, Guy, 151, 153

Lalonde, Newsy, 137
Lambert, Yvon, 153
Landry, Tom, 155, 158, 159,
    166–69, 172, 173–79, 229, 231,
    232, 233
Lane, Frank, 212
Lansing Laurels, 183
Lapointe, Guy, 153
La Porte Cubs, 209
Larkin, Dick, 228
Laycoe, Hal, 143
Lazzeri, Tony, 11
Lee, Greg, 100
Lemaire, Jacques, 153
Lemon, Bob, 11
Lilly, Bob, 174–79
Logan, Jerry, 79
Lombardi, Vince, 109, 121, 167,
    169, 196, 231, 232
Looney, Joe Don, 162–63
Lopat, Ed, 18, 28, 35
LoPiano, Donna, 191, 192
Los Angeles Dodgers, 6, 203
Los Angeles Lakers, 49, 55–61,
    100
Los Angeles Rams, 6, 49, 63, 69,
    75, 79, 158, 160, 162, 173,
    226–27
Louisiana State University, 81
Louisville, University of, 75
Lucas, Jerry, 49

Macauley, Ed, 50
McCafferty, Don, 78
McCarter Andrew, 106, 107
McCarthy, Joe, 24, 25, 26, 30,
    231, 232
McDaniels, David, 162
McGill, Bill, 49
McHugh, Howie, 43, 50–52
McIntosh, Doug, 90
Mack, Connie, 217
McKinney, Bones, 47
McMahon, Mike, 141
MacPhail, Larry, 22–24, 26
MacPhail, Lee, 22

Mallory, Bill, 118
Mangual, Angel, 222
Mantle, Mickey, 18–20, 28, 29, 34,
    224, 229
Marchibroda, Ted, 84
Maris, Roger, 28
Marshall, Don, 139
Marshall, Ralph, 139
Martin, Billy, 28, 39
Matte, Tom, 65
Maxvill, Dal, 33, 206, 222
Mays, Willie, 10, 34, 36, 228
Meredith, Don, 169, 170, 173
Miami College, 128, 129
Miami Dolphins, 4, 62–63, 78, 79,
    156, 172
Michigan, University of, 113, 115,
    118, 130
Michigan State University, 115
Michigan Wolverines, 94–96
Mikan, George, 104
Milwaukee Braves, 207
Milwaukee Bucks, 100
Minnesota Vikings, 3–4, 63, 79,
    156, 171, 172, 173
"Mississippi Gambler." See Unitas,
    John
Monday, Rick, 221
Montreal Canadiens, 5, 87,
    134–53, 227–28, 229, 233
Moore, Dickie, 139
Morenz, Howie, 137
Morton, Craig, 173
Mosdel, Ken, 139
Mossi, Don, 11
Murchison, Clint, 157–58, 166
Murphy, "Fireman" Johnny, 11
Murphy, Franklin, 108
Musial, Stan, 10, 228
Myers, David, 106

Namath, Joe, 69
Narleski, Ray, 11
Nater, Sven, 100–4
National Basketball Association
    (NBA), 40, 41, 47, 50, 104, 111

National Collegiate Athletic
  Association (NCAA), 87, 89,
  90, 96, 98, 100, 106, 107, 112
National Football League (NFL),
  62, 63, 64, 71, 75, 81, 154,
  156–58, 160, 161, 166, 168,
  169, 226, 227
National Hockey League (NHL),
  136, 137, 145
National League, 203
Nelson, Don, 49, 60
New Orleans Saints, 162
New York Giants, 62, 64, 166,
  167, 171
New York Jets, 69, 78
New York Knicks, 57, 58
New York Mets, 26, 36, 220
New York Yankees, 4, 5, 9–39,
  45, 87, 110, 137, 166, 181, 182,
  203, 205, 207, 217, 221, 224,
  227, 228, 230, 233
Nielson, Jim, 99
Nikolic, Aleksandar, 96
Norman, Pettis, 164
North, Bill, 222
North Carolina College, 47
North Carolina State University,
  106, 118
Northwestern University, 118
Notre Dame, 113, 118
Notre Dame Fighting Irish, 106

Oakland A's, 9, 33, 36, 203–24,
  228–33
Oakland Raiders, 3, 63, 71, 173
Odom, Blue Moon, 205–6, 221
Ohio State Buckeyes, 5, 65, 73,
  113–33, 228, 233
Ohio State University, 49, 96
Ohio University, 118
Oilers, 166
Olmstead, Bert, 139
Orange Lionettes, 188, 190, 191
Ouachita Baptist, 164

Parker, Jim, 64, 73–75, 77–79,

116–18, 122–23, 130
Parseghian, Ara, 118
Patterson, Steve, 100
Paul, Gabe, 36
Pearson, Monte, 13
Pearson, Ron, 108
Penn State, 113
Pepitone, Joe, 28
Philadelphia Athletics, 209, 211
Philadelphia Eagles, 162, 171
Philadelphia Warriors, 55, 57, 58,
  111
Phoenix Suns, 41–42
Pittsburgh Steelers, 62–63, 75, 156
Plante, Jacques, 139
"Playoff Bowl," 168–69
Pollack, Sam, 150
Pont, John, 118
Portland Trail Blazers, 104, 111
Provost, Claude, 139
Prugh, Jeff, 96
Pugh, Jethro, 164
Purdue University, 107

Quesnel, Beth, 199–201

Raschi, Vic, 28, 33–34, 224
Raybestos Brakettes, 5, 181–202,
  228–29, 231, 233
Raymond, Ralph, 182–84, 187,
  192–99, 201, 228, 231, 232
Reardon, Kenny, 137
Redskins, 173
Reeves, Dan, 75, 158–60
Reinalda, Barbara, 186, 201–2
Reynolds, Allie, 28, 31, 224
Richard, Henri "The Pocket," 137,
  139
Richard, Maurice "Rocket," 135,
  137, 139–43, 145, 148, 149,
  150, 153, 228, 230–31
Richardson, Bobby, 18–20, 23, 28,
  30, 31, 35, 224
Rizzuto, Phil, 28, 35, 224
Robertson, Oscar, 54
Robinson, Jackie, 34

Rockne, Knute, 109
Rolfe, Red, 11
Rose, Pete, 229
Rose Bowl, 118
Rosenbloom, Carroll, 73–75, 78, 79, 85, 227, 228, 233
Rowe, Curtis, 99, 100, 101
Rudi, Joe, 207, 217, 221, 223
Ruel, Claude, 150
Ruffing, Red, 11, 12
Rupert, "Jake," 20, 22
Russel, Bill, 47, 49–55, 57, 58, 59–61, 104, 229–31
Russell, Cazzie, 94, 96
Ruth, Babe, 1, 9, 217, 228

St. Louis Browns, 211
St. Louis Cardinals, 10, 33, 171, 172, 206
Sanders, Tom, 49
San Francisco State, 7, 49, 171, 172
Saperstein, Abe, 50
Savard, Serge, 153
Sayers, Gale, 228
Schembechler, Bo, 118
Schramm, Texas E., 158, 160, 163, 166, 169, 174
Schumacher, Diane, 186
Scott, Charlie, 44–45
Selke, Frank, 150
Selkirk, George "Twinkletoes," 11, 12–15, 16, 17, 35
Shackleford, Lynn, 98, 99
Sheehy, "Big Pete," 39
Shinnick, Don, 67, 79
Shula, Don, 67–69, 70, 78, 79, 231
Shutt, Steve, 153
Siegfried, Larry, 49, 58
Simpson, O. J., 7, 179
Simpson, William S., 186, 187, 188, 193, 201
Slaughter, Fred, 90
Southern California Trojans, 6, 98, 113
Stagg, Amos Alonzo, 114

Stanford University, 93
Stanley Cup, 112, 134, 137, 141, 142, 150
Starr, Bart, 171, 230
Staubach, Roger, 164, 165, 173, 176
Steinbrenner, George, 36, 227
Stengel, Casey, 9, 26, 27–33, 36, 224, 231, 232, 233
Stock, Wes, 223
Strahan, Kathy, 183–84, 196–99
Sun City Saints, 192
Super Bowl, 3, 4, 62, 63, 69, 71, 78, 79, 81, 112, 154, 156, 157, 169–71, 172, 180, 231
Szymanski, Dick, 65, 67, 68, 77–78, 79, 81

Tarkenton, Fran, 75
Tenace, Gene, 207, 221
Texas Western, 96
Thomas, Joe, 79–81, 85
Thompson, Cliff, 143
Thompson, David, 106
Tickey, Bertha Reagan, 188–93, 195–96, 230
Topping, Dan, 20, 22, 24, 26, 34
Toronto Maple Leafs, 139, 141, 149
Trgovich, Pete, 106

UCLA Bruins, 5, 6, 87–112, 126, 129, 228, 233
Unitas, Johnny, 64–66, 73, 75–78, 79, 81, 85, 86, 162, 173, 228, 233
United States Olympic team, 100
University of Pittsburgh, 179

Vallely, John, 100
Veeck, Bill, 211
Vezina, Georges, 137
Vogel, Bob, 69–71, 72, 73, 78–79, 114, 123, 126, 129, 131

Wake Forest, 47–49

Walker, Chet, 55
Walton, Bill, 104–6, 111, 112, 230
Warner, Glenn "Pop," 1, 114
Warren, Mike, 98, 99
Warriner, Diane, 192
Washington, Claudell, 207, 221
Washington, Kenny, 90
Washington, Richard, 106
Waterfield, Bob, 75
Webb, Del, 20, 22, 24, 26, 34
Weiss, George, 13, 22, 24, 26, 34, 36
West, Jerry, 55, 58, 59, 61, 228
Whittier Gold Sox, 190
Wicks, Sidney, 99, 100, 101, 111
Widby, Ron, 164
Wilkes, Keith, 100, 102

Williams, Carroll, 104
Williams, Ted, 10, 12, 228
Wooden, John, 91, 93–95, 96, 99, 100, 107–12, 126, 228, 231–33
Woodling, Gene, 28, 30–35, 224, 230
Woolpert, Phil, 50
World Hockey Association, 136
World Series, 4, 6, 7, 9, 10, 15, 35, 36, 112, 166, 205, 206, 210, 220, 222
Wright, Rayfield, 164
Wynn, Early, 11

Yale University, 118, 164
Yawkey, Tom, 3